WRITERS AND THEIR WORK

ISOBEL ARMSTRONG
General Editor

MACBETH

William Shakespeare

MACBETH

Kathleen E. McLuskie

NORTHCOTE
BRITISH COUNCIL

First published in 2009 by Northcote House Publishers Ltd, Horndon House, Horndon, Devon PL19 9NQ, United Kingdom.
Tel: +44 (01822) 810066 Fax: +44 (01822) 810034.

British Library Cataloguing-in-Publication Data
A catalogue record for this book is available from the British Library

ISBN 978-0-7463-1148-7 hardcover
ISBN 978-0-7463-0843-1 paperback

Typeset by PDQ Typesetting, Newcastle-under-Lyme
Printed and bound in the United Kingdom

Contents

Acknowledgements

This book arose out of my complete failure to submit to the disciplines of editing the play. I am grateful to Richard Proudfoot and Pamela Mason for their generosity and forbearance during that process. Its final form was inspired by a holiday conversation with a Shakespeare enthusiast who became my model audience. My colleagues and students at the Shakespeare Institute have set a standard for ways of talking about Shakespeare. Jean Howard, Richard Dutton and Peter Holland have been interested enough in the work to publish essays that helped me develop its key ideas and David and my daughters have tolerated my obsession with the play over many years. To all of them I am grateful.

References

All quotations from *Macbeth* are from the modern spelling edition of A.R. Braunmuller, *The New Cambridge Shakespeare*, (Cambridge: Cambridge University Press, 1997).

Introduction:
The Writer and his Work

A writer and his work, Shakespeare and *Macbeth*: the connection seems straightforward enough. The writer, William Shakespeare, is connected to the work, *Macbeth*, by the publication of *Macbeth* in the first printed collection of *Mr William Shakespeare's Comedies, Histories and Tragedies Published according to the True Originall Copies*, the so-called First Folio published in 1623, a decade after Shakespeare's death. The four hundred years that stand between that connection and the present have, however, complicated their relationship.

We know more about Shakespeare, the playwright from Stratford-upon-Avon, than we do about many early-modern writers, in spite of the tantalizing gaps that remain in the chronology of his life. But when we try to invoke that life to explain the work, we encounter not only an early-modern writer but the mythologized giant of western literature, the source of the stories that structure our perception of the world, whose lines are quoted, by those who know them, to sum-up experiences of love or tyranny, nature or death. The writer's reputation depends upon the works and the works are, for the most part, the primary evidence for his thoughts about the world in which he lived. The precise nature of the connection between the man from Stratford and the plays attributed to him has been a source of endless speculation. His life is recorded (as it is for most early modern people) only in official documents and accounts of financial transactions. This leaves the scholar and admirer of Shakespeare's plays to track the relationship between their sense of the creativity that informs his plays and the information about the times in which he lived, the theatrical

1

profession in which he worked and the print industry that produced the texts that remain the only trace of his work.

Inevitably, there has been, since the late nineteenth century, a reaction against this towering reputation. Shakespeare's claim to the authorship of his plays has been called into question by professional scholars as well as extraordinarily tenacious generations of anti-bardolators.[1] This book will assume that *Macbeth* was written by Shakespeare and that, by close attention to the extant text of the play, we can come to understand something of his working practices and the way that he drew on the ideas of his time and the theatrical resources at his disposal to create it.

The 'work', of course, is not straightforward. It is rare for readers and audiences to encounter it in the form in which it appeared in 1623. It has been edited, anthologized, adapted, turned into a novel, played as a political skit, as film, and as opera. Perhaps inevitably, it has also been mocked and travestied; readers and audiences may have first become aware of it because of its, often quoted, famous lines: 'out damned spot' or 'Is this a dagger that I see before me'.[2] These enormously varied forms and versions of *Macbeth* all raise questions about what the 'work' is: is it the Folio text of *Macbeth*? Is it the (lost) manuscript that Shakespeare (presumably) gave to the players? Is it a performance of the play in Shakespeare's time? Or is it the sum of all the productions of the play that have occurred in the intervening 400 years?

These questions about what *Macbeth* is lie behind every discussion of the work, whether or not they are explicitly stated. They arise because, in the case of Shakespeare and *Macbeth*, the relationship between the writer and his work was called into question in the very process of publication that turned a play into a work. When Shakespeare's fellow players, Hemmings and Condell, collected his plays into the great Folio volume of 1623, it was unusual for plays to appear in folio form. Shakespeare's contemporary Ben Jonson had had his existing plays collected into a folio in 1616 and the oddity of a playwright claiming that 'his plays are his works', was mocked in the poetry that greeted the publication.[3] Ben Jonson wrote commendatory verses for the Shakespeare collection and he was at pains to insist that 'what he hath left us' were works of art that could stand comparison

2

with the ancient poets and outshone the achievements of his contemporary dramatists. He insisted, moreover, that the plays would survive because they had been printed and could be appreciated by discerning readers:

> Thou art a monument without a tomb,
> And art alive still while thy book doth live,
> And we have wits to read and praise to give.[4]

Ben Jonson made a distinction between the praise of 'all men's suffrage' that the plays gained in performance and the more discriminating praise that they would attract in print. In doing so he began to open the gap between the play in performance and the printed work; between the originating moment of the plays' first production and the work's continuing value 'for all time' that would depend on readers' judgement.

It is perhaps surprising to discover that the 1623 Folio text of *Macbeth* is perfectly accessible to a modern reader. It is printed in two columns with such typographical conventions of early printing as the long 's' and the interchangeability of 'u' and 'v'. Its spelling and punctuation are slightly different from modern practice and were often altered in later editions but these typographical conventions seldom present serious problems in understanding the lines.

Where subsequent editors have most often altered the text is in altering the lineation (the way that the text is set out in lines) of the 1623 text into more regular blank verse. The apparent (but infrequent) irregularity of the verse may have been because of the printing house practice of dividing the text between two typesetters (called compositors) rather than printing it sequentially. This meant that the text did not always neatly fit the page. If too much text had to be squashed into a page, verse might be printed as prose to save space. If not enough text remained to fill the page, the text might be broken into more lines.[5] Since most readers first get to know the play in a modern edition, the Folio lineation sometimes seems odd but the text as a whole seldom presents the kind of syntactic or verbal muddle that is occasionally encountered in Shakespeare's other plays.

The individual 'work', *Macbeth*, was also created by the Folio collection. Unlike many of Shakespeare's plays, *Macbeth* had never been printed before and, as we shall see, the record of its life in the theatre presented a rather different version of the play in its own time as well as in subsequent performances. Readers who opened the Folio at F 131, where the text begins, would have faced a new text that, like all play texts, required an imaginative process in order to turn the words on the page into imagined action.

By 1623, the publication of plays was sufficiently well established to suggest that the process of reading plays was fairly common. The stage directions gave some sense of their life in the theatre but there is some evidence plays were also read for the poetry or the sententious ideas that could be copied out as Edward Pudsey did into his commonplace book.[6] The modern link between the play and the work, the efforts to read a play so that imagined action turns reading into visualized performance or interpretation may have been less common.

The transformation of the play into a 'work' played a vital part in making the play available to subsequent audiences and readers. Although the play had an extended afterlife on the stage from the Restoration onward, without the transformation into a printed work, it could have had no life at all. The connection between the play and the work also took place in time: more than a decade had passed since it was first performed. That relationship between the experience of reading the work and the past of its performance was a critical aspect of the experience of *Macbeth* from its first appearance as a work. In modern times, the relationship between the work and its theatrical past is rather different. Its 'pastness' is sometimes seen as a barrier to its appreciation by a modern audience, because of the strangeness of language and ideas from the past. The same 'pastness', however is also a significant element in the value that is placed on the work, the sense that it provides an opportunity to engage with a work that has transcended time. Most paradoxically of all, the gap in time between the play and the work that existed at the time of the First Folio has, in modern times been reversed as audiences engage with the play through the recurrent innovation of theatrical productions.

Performance always takes place in the present, yet behind every revival or adaptation there lurks the tradition of past performances that are either embraced or rejected by the performance being experienced. The connection between the present of performance and the past of the work is always in question, whether history is used to validate the modern experience of the play or defiantly rejected in search of a modern relevance that can overcome the 'pastness' of the play's original language or the circumstances of its historical existence.

The recurring tensions between the 'pastness' of the work and the immediacy of the play, between the experience of drama and the awareness of the history that haunts it, are often resolved by invoking a naïve reader, spontaneously responding to the play's inherent power.[7] Yet that sense of the play's inherent power is itself a result of the cumulative effect of centuries of reading and theatrical reproduction that have moulded *Macbeth* into a coherent work of art. Critical, editorial and theatrical interventions have both identified, and solved, a set of problems with the play. Questions of Macbeth's motivation and moral responsibility, or the nature of witchcraft, or the significance of renaissance ideas of kingship have been identified as part of the meaning of the work. These recurring critical questions have contributed to the process of turning the play into a work that rewards interpretation and thus ensures its continuing fascination.

When we approach the work as readers we bring those expectations of meaning with us. In order to engage with the work as a work, we must enter an imaginative process that turns the words on the page into meaning. Because the text provides only speeches and stage directions, we must move from those speeches and stage directions into narrative and imagined action. That imaginative and intellectual process can then lead on to interpretation that reinforces (or sometimes undermines) our sense of the play as a valued work of art. When we experience the play as an audience in the theatre, the process of turning the words into narrative is often partly complete. Directors have taken decisions about costume, physical appearance and tone of voice so that the play can be enjoyed as an experience in the theatre. However, when we are aware of the work behind the play, we are offered an additional pleasure of setting existing knowledge against the new experience on offer. Once more, the sense that the play is a work with infinite potential for meaning is reinforced and its value reaffirmed.

Engaging with 'the writer and his work', then, requires more than presenting another interpretation, or even the summary of past interpretations. It involves opening out a complex process that begins with an alert attention to the mix of the familiar and the strange presented by the Folio text of *Macbeth,* in order to see the work as a set of literary and theatrical effects. It continues with an awareness of the sources and origins of those effects in the narrative and theatrical resources at the writer's disposal and the ways in which the writer worked with those resources in the plays that preceded *Macbeth.* This combination of the text and its raw materials proves a method for understanding the link between the writer and his work. Another step is required, however, if we are to understand the process of making that past relationship available to the present readers. That is to identify the layers of the past that go to make up the modern *Macbeth*: the combination of critical interest in ethical issues, the psychology of character and the politics of kingship as well as the ways that those interests have informed modern productions to make them live again.

All of these different interests have made *Macbeth* and Shakespeare, the work and the writer what they are in modern times. However the continued existence and significance of the writer and his work also depends upon the terms in which they are made available to their readers and audiences.

The tension between the play and the work that existed from their first reproduction in the 1623 Folio has shifted and changed over the centuries. At this point in the early twenty-first century, it is shifting again. In the twentieth century, the cultural value that Shakespeare's work was thought to embody was institutionalized in school and university curricula and in state-supported theatre as a means of making it more accessible to the whole nation. This process has continued into the twenty-first century but questions about the educational value of the culture of the past, together with new technologies of access have changed the nature of the 'work' on offer. If eight-year-old children encounter *Macbeth* in a cartoon and then produce their own performance, if the play is rewritten for a television production or adapted with new settings by an international theatre company, are we dealing with the play or the work? Does the significance of the work depend on its continuing association with its writer or did his role end when he handed over the manuscript to the players some time in the first decade of the seventeenth century?

6

1

The Work and the Story

The process of reading the text in order to turn it into a story produces these complex connections between the play and the work. The Folio text names the characters and their speeches with occasional stage directions and the reader has to connect them to create a narrative out of the imagined action. For example, the opening stage direction of the Folio text reads *'Thunder and Lightning. Enter three Witches'*. It presents a characteristic combination of a sound effect and figures on the stage. At this stage in the text, the reader is given no hint about what 'witches' are and in spite of the overload of meaning and commentary that they have received, it is important to hold off from interpretation in order to see how the Folio text (rather than subsequent interpretative theatre productions) structures the information that it provides and the range of effects it makes possible.

The opening line begins with an interrogative: 'When?' It rhymes with 'again' and the rhyme reinforces the idea of repetition. Immediately we are drawn into the time-frame of the play: the past of the witches' meeting, the present of the 'hurley burley' (not a common expression before Shakespeare used it) and a future that will involve someone called 'Macbeth'. In performance, of course, the costume and style of the witches could communicate much more. However those choices of costume and style are matters of directorial intent and throughout the play's long production history, they have pre-empted the reading of the play with presentations that were distracting, if not tendentious. The reader, on the other hand, can keep a more open mind, following the information that the text provides in its own time.

In the following scene, Act 1, Scene 2, we are given a new perspective on the 'battle lost and won' and the exploits of Macbeth. King Duncan hears Macbeth praised by the wounded sergeant, a much clearer form of reportage than the witches' puzzling allusions. Once again, the past affects the future, as Duncan responds to the wounded sergeant's story by stripping the traitorous Thane of Cawdor of his title and conferring it on Macbeth. All this information about the action's past, present and future is gathered before Macbeth and Banquo appear in the next scene. They enter onto the witches' meeting and immediately ask the question that readers have been puzzling over since the first line of the play:

> What are these,
> So withered, and so wild in their attire,
> That look not like th'inhabitants o'th' earth,
> And yet are on't? – Live you, or are you aught
> That man may question? You seem to understand me,
> By each at once her choppy finger laying
> Upon her skinny lips: you should be women,
> And yet your beards forbid me to interpret
> That you are so.

> (1.3.37–45)

The reader, however, already has more knowledge than Macbeth and Banquo. Having seen Duncan's actions in the previous scene, s/he is not surprised by the witches' first two greetings to Macbeth, which hail him as Thane of Glamis and then Thane of Cawdor. The lurch into an unexpected future comes with the third greeting: 'All hail Macbeth, that shalt be king hereafter'.

In order for the narrative pleasure of suspense to be fulfilled, the reader must be prepared to believe the witches and the Folio text allows ample time for that belief to build. By engaging the reader in the witches' past, present and future, presented in the opening lines of the play, and by then providing the army's perspective on the action, the text allows the reader to be engaged in the story's forward movement. In those first three scenes, the text provides a little more information about the witches and in doing so, it opens a gap between the reader's knowledge and that of Banquo and Macbeth.

After the witches have spoken to Macbeth and Banquo, the stage direction reads 'Witches vanish 'and they puzzle over what

8

they have seen and heard:

> BANQUO. The earth hath bubbles, as the water has,
> And these are of them. Whither are they vanished?
> MACBETH. Into the air, and what seemed corporal,
> Melted, as breath into the wind. Would they had stayed.
> BANQUO. Were such things here as we do speak about?
> Or have we eaten on the insane root,
> That takes the reason prisoner?
>
> (1.3.77–83)

Macbeth's and Banquo's baffled questions offer alternative interpretations of what they have seen. The witches are compared with puzzling natural phenomena: the way water bubbles disperse or the way breath disappears in the wind. Alternatively, Banquo suggests, they might be an hallucination induced by inadvertently eating a mind-altering root.

In the theatre, Macbeth's and Banquo's confusion need not be endorsed by the action. In performance the witches need not literally vanish: they have almost ten lines to get off the stage. Their encounter with Macbeth and Banquo, not only provides the information that will carry the action forward; it also opens up the gap between what is shown on stage and the critically different interpretations that the characters bring to it.

The reader's knowledge of the witches' truth is further contrasted with Macbeth's reaction to them. He sees their prophecy as a moral paradox that 'Cannot be ill; cannot be good', setting known events as a counterpoint to a moral analysis and he ends his first consideration of the prophecy with a stoical acceptance of the workings of fate:

> If chance will have me king, why chance may crown me,
> Without my stir.
>
> (1.3.142–3)

The lineation of the Folio text, regularized into ten syllable lines in most modern editions, separates off the three concepts into discrete events. However, the action of the narrative prevents that separation. Duncan's election of his eldest son, the Prince of Cumberland, to be his heir, closes off the possibility of a chance fulfilment of the witches' prophecy and leaves the connection to Macbeth. His translation of prophecy into regicidal ambition, 'that suggestion,/ Whose horrid image doth unfix my hair',

9

appears to be based in a logical extension from known 'truths' but the truths told by the witches and the truth of moral action are driven apart as the play proceeds.

The distinction between the witches' action and the characters' interpretation of it, in some measure accounts for their critical role in the play that has produced commentary out of all proportion to the amount of time they take up in reading or performance. Within the play's structure they constitute a dramatic device that increases the suspense, drives the narrative to its conclusion and keeps the audience on tenterhooks about how the action will be resolved. Achieving this theatrical end requires only three strategically placed scenes: at the beginning to start the action and alert the audience to the importance of Macbeth who will not appear for another two scenes; towards the end of Act 1 to deliver the all important message to Macbeth and Banquo – a message which carries the action through the murders of Duncan and Banquo; and again in Act 4 to provide a new momentum which will drive the suspense through to the play's climax.

Their action in the play divides the narrative into three movements. In the first, from the witches' prophecy to the murder of Duncan, attention is focused on Macbeth's agonized contemplation of the murder and his wife's eager embrace of the witches' prophecy. In the second, from the murder of Duncan to Macbeth's return to the witches, we witness the hero's realization that his triumph is fatally compromised by the second part of the witches' prophecy – that Banquo's heirs will succeed Macbeth. He attempts and fails to thwart their prophecy by killing Banquo and is forced to contemplate the horror of that failure by the appearance of Banquo's ghost. In the third, the action moves from Scotland to England and back as Macbeth's enemies prepare their revenge.

The witches' final scene, in Act 4, provides a new momentum that carries the action through to the play's climax. In Act 4, Scene 1, the enigmatic creatures of the first act, who speak in riddles and then vanish, are given a more extended dramatic sequence that demonstrates a power quite different from the village witchcraft of killing swine or tormenting the sailor's wife. They conjure up apparitions that emblematize Macbeth's sense of his own power and his fatal vulnerability. The first three apparitions are of *'an armed Head'*, *'a bloody Child'* and *'a Child crowned, with a tree in his hand'* (4.1.67; 4.1.75; 4.1.84).

The armed head tells Macbeth that he should 'Beware the Thane of Fife'; the bloody child that he need fear nothing since 'none of woman born/Shall harm Macbeth' (4.1.79-80) and the third apparition – *'a Child Crowned, with a tree in his hand'* that

> Macbeth shall never vanquished be until
> Great Birnam Wood to high Dunsinane Hill
> Shall come against him.

> (4.1.91–3)

Each apparition is accompanied by *Thunder*, the witches' signature sound effect. It speaks its prophecy and then *'Descends'* probably through the trap door on the stage. When the apparitions are gone, the cauldron also sinks through the stage and *Hautboyes*, loud wind instruments, herald *'A show of eight kings, and [the] last, with a glass in his hand [Banquo's Ghost following]'*.[1]

None of these apparitions requires special effects beyond the music and the means for descent. Their particular impact on the play depends upon the way they offer possibilities for the future outcome of the story and, above all, by their carefully orchestrated effect in Macbeth himself.

The effects on Macbeth are carefully paced. The first apparition confirms Macbeth's suspicion of Macduff: 'Thou hast harped my fear aright'. (4.1.71) The second reassures him further but increases his resolve to 'make assurance double sure /And take a bond of fate' (4.1.82). The third makes him confident that he 'Shall live the lease of nature' (4.1.98), his natural life-span. This confident sense of a hold on the future is almost immediately troubled by Macbeth's memory of Banquo's prophecy. He asks 'shall Banquo's issue ever/Reign in this kingdom?' (4.1.101–2), and is then appalled by the appearance of the procession of kings that stretch out from the figure of Banquo to an unending future seen in the mirror that Banquo carries.

Throughout the scene, the witches are in control: Macbeth is forced into the role of watching the audience by their constant calls for both silence and attention. The audience in the theatre, on the other hand, sees both the apparitions and the initial

11

defiant increase in Macbeth's confidence followed by his anguished collapse as he realizes the implications of the procession of kings. Macbeth's reactions place the show of apparitions into the context of the play's larger narrative. The events of the play proceed inexorably while Macbeth, again and again, seeks to bargain with fate and stand in the way of a known future. Just before the procession of kings appears, the witches chant

> Show his eyes, and grieve his heart,
> Come like shadows, so depart

(4.1.109–10)

The representation of the kings, like the witches in the first act or Banquo's ghost, will wound Macbeth's heart for he cannot simply contemplate the vision that the witches produce. Macbeth's commentary not only tells us what he sees but also gives meaning to what is represented on the stage by his horrified reaction. He confronts the final apparition with

> Thou art too like the spirit of *Banquo*. Down!
> Thy crown does sear mine eyeballs. And thy hair,
> Thou other gold-bound-brow, is like the first:
> A third, is like the former. – Filthy hags,
> Why do you show me this? – A fourth? Start, eyes!
> What, will the line stretch out to'th' crack of doom?
> Another yet? A seventh? I'll see no more.
> And yet the eighth appears, who bears a glass,
> Which shows me many more. And some I see,
> That two-fold balls, and treble scepters carry.
> Horrible sight!

(4.1.111–21)

All the defiant calm of his response to the prophecies of the future is gone. The final apparition connects the present, the past and the future. It gestures towards a future beyond the play when Banquo's heirs will reign, it reminds Macbeth (and the audience) of the prophecy about Banquo's heirs and, in the figure of Banquo's ghost, it dramatizes the complete failure of Macbeth's attempt to turn prophecy aside by his own violent action.

By contrasting the physical effects on stage with Macbeth's reaction to them, the apparition scene highlights the contrast between the play's forward movement and Macbeth's desperate efforts to control them. Each time the witches appear in the play, they offer a possibility for the development of the action; each time Macbeth responds with an attempt to turn their prophecies to his advantage. This final appearance again offers three possibilities for the ensuing action. It creates suspense about how the action might be resolved and in Macbeth's combined response of over-confidence and impotent rage, it prefigures the disastrous consequences of his attempt to 'take a bond of fate'.

Macbeth's resolve is directly mocked in the immediate stage actin. He is confident that he can 'tell pale-hearted fear it lies, / And sleep in spite of thunder' (4.1.84–5). His words are echoed by a thunderclap that mocks his certainty. His confidence that he will be able to sleep, offers an ironic reminder of the voice that had haunted him after Duncan's murder, crying '"Sleep no more" . . . "Glamis hath murdered sleep, and therefore Cawdor / Shall sleep no more: Macbeth shall sleep no more"' (2.2.45–6).

At the end of the scene, both because of and in spite of the witches' new predictions, Macbeth moves against Macduff, the Thane of Fife, murdering his wife and children. That action triggers Macduff's revenge and gives an emotional as well as narrative impetus to the last part of the play. But Macduff's ensuing vengeful crusade, supported by the English forces, is complicated by the conundrum of Macbeth's magical immunity from harm. The structuring of the play's final scenes spins out the suspense as the English army approaches, fulfilling each prophecy in turn and providing space for its implications to sink in. By oscillating between the Scots and English camps, the structure also offers a contrasting commentary between Macduff's cause and the desperate, violent rage of Macbeth's final struggle. Macbeth's final defeat is not achieved just by the witches' trickery of moving forests or the unknown implications of Macduff's Caesarean birth. It is carefully managed to contrast the heroic comradeship of the English forces with Macbeth's isolated, enraged and reckless courage.

In the English camp, Siward, the leader of the joint English and Scots forces, and Malcolm, Duncan's son, calmly observe that Macbeth has resolved to sit out a siege even though his forces are leaving him: 'none serve with him, but constrained things / Whose hearts are absent too' (5.4.13–14). Their intelligence is confirmed as the action switches to Macbeth's preparation for the English force's arrival. Macbeth has retreated to the physically and psychically safe ground of his castle's strength and the witches' final prophecy. In spite of his eloquent defiance, he recognizes that he is losing support:

> here let them lie,
> Till famine and the ague eat them up.
> Were they not forced with those that should be ours,
> We might have met them dareful, beard to beard,
> And beat them backward home. What is that noise?

(5.5.3–7)

But this defiance is immediately checked by '*A cry within of women*' and the news of his wife's death that provokes Macbeth's terrible (and now famous) contemplation of the futility of a life that consists of no more than the dreadful round of tomorrow and tomorrow and tomorrow.

The text keeps the action moving, driven by the prophecies, but that forward movement is counterpointed by Macbeth's growing despair. This complex emotional preamble to the news that Birnam Wood is come to Dunsinane lifts the news from a banal corroboration of the prophecy to the first tipping point of the finale. Macbeth's fury at the soldier's news is moderated by his recognition that his end may be in sight. He tells the soldier:

> If thou speak'st false,
> Upon the next tree shall thou hang alive
> Till Famine cling thee; if thy speech be sooth,
> I care not if thou dost for me as much.

(5.5.37–40)

For the first time, and even before the prophecies have been worked through, he begins to doubt the witches:

> I pull in resolution and begin
> To doubt th'equivocation of the fiend,
> That lies like truth

(5.5.41–3)

His initial interpretation of the witches, that had depended on inductive reason, working from 'two truths' or the physical observation of the apparitions, begins to fail him. He now uses the term 'equivocation', meaning riddling or telling half truths.

14

He also refers to the witches as 'the fiend' or the devil. However, his doubt only increases his courage. He recognizes that if the witches' prophecy can be fulfilled by equivocation, 'There is nor flying hence, nor tarrying here'. The only solution is in action:

> ...Arm, arm and out! [i.e. of the castle]
>
> . . . . .
>
> ...Blow wind, come wrack;
> At least we'll die with harness on our back.
>
> (5.5.45, 50–1)

The resolution of the last prophecy, about Birnam wood, moves the narrative forward in providing the motivation for Macbeth to break the siege. It creates the opportunity for the extended battle scene that builds excitement for the culminating confrontation between Macbeth and Macduff. In spite of Macbeth's rejection of the witches' truth, their influence on the narrative extends right up until this final scene. When Macduff tells him of his own magical birth: 'Macduff was from his mother's womb/Untimely ripped' (5.8.15–16), that final, triumphant endorsement of the witches' last prophecy forces Macbeth finally to confront the gap between the truth of the witches' prophecy and his own potential for action.

The pacing of that realization is brilliantly slowed down. Macbeth is initially dismayed:

> Accursed be that tongue that tells me so;
> For it hath cowed my better part of man;
> And be these juggling fiends no more believed,
> That palter with us in a double sense,
> That keep the word of promise to our ear
> And break it to our hope. I'll not fight with thee.
>
> (5.8.17–22)

Behind that speech lies a century of controversy over the efficacy of prophecy and the power of witches. Its theatrical force, however, depends on the primary aesthetic pleasure of a narrative stopped in its tracks, of an ending which both had to be and might not have been. The significance of the literally show-stopping moment is enlarged and extended by the speech's language and structure. The mysterious witches, described with such curiosity and speculation by Macbeth and Banquo, and seen as the source of reassurance after Macbeth has

15

faced Banquo's ghost in Act 3, Scene 4, are denounced as 'juggling fiends' when his faith in them evaporates. And the antitheses in the final couplet between 'keep' and 'break', 'ear' and 'hope' potentially apply, beyond the particular case of Macbeth, to every failure of aspiration or wishful thinking.

Macduff's challenge to Macbeth breaks the moment of reflection. It returns the action to a conflict between men, a conflict that Macbeth responds to with a heroic denial of the inevitable, fighting to the last in a duel which offers both exciting physical display and an image of an elemental conflict between good and evil. That division between good and evil is paradoxical to the last. Macduff has the moral authority of the avenging victim of Macbeth's murderous aggression. However, the attention that the play has given to Macbeth's psychic and ethical torment, together with the courage of his final stand, compromise a simple attribution of moral judgement and create the sense of ethical and aesthetic complexity that have kept the reader's interest through the action.

2

The Writer's Tools: Action and Language

The sense of aesthetic and ethical complexity that critics and audiences have admired in *Macbeth* is, then, an effect of the play's dramatic structure: the double movement of the witches' prophecies and Macbeth's efforts to turn them to his own advantage. The narrative moves from the fulfilment of one prophecy with Duncan's murder, through Macbeth's attempt to thwart the second prophecy by killing Banquo. The terrifying appearance of Banquo's ghost, however, dramatizes Macbeth's insecurity and he seeks 'to know/By the worst means the worst' (3.4.134). His final encounter with the witches, however, confirms his suspicions about Macduff and the supernatural assurances of the witches' new prophecies move the narrative from king-killing to revenge.

All of this narrative and dramatic complexity is achieved with the resources of language and the simplest of physical effects available on the early modern stage. Subsequent commentary and theatre productions have filled in the gaps that this simplicity leaves in the narrative and interpretation of the play, but by reading the text alone, it is possible to see how those gaps are made and how they leave open the spaces into which interpretation has entered the reading of the play.

One of the most important effects of the Folio text is the way it manages the relationship between what is shown on stage and the way it creates a world beyond the stage that presses both upon the action and on the imagination of the principal actors. In the early part of the play, the off-stage world is presented in familiar and conventional ways. In Act 1, Scene 2, the bloody sergeant who brings the news of battle presents a version of the 'messenger speech' that Shakespeare and others had learned from Senecan drama. The figure that delivers it never appears again and his report, for all its rhetorical elaboration, has scant purchase on the subsequent action. In contrast, as we have seen, the witches' brief invocation of their earlier meetings and ambiguous prophecies are central to the unfolding story, even though they are off-stage for most of the play.

This balance between off-stage and on-stage action is an important source of the play's dramatic effects: it allows an intense focus on the principal characters but it also places them in a world which seems mysterious because it is never seen on stage and invites critical speculation because the play gives its readers so little to go on. In the action leading up to Duncan's murder, the king himself scarcely appears. He is welcomed at the castle gate by Macbeth's lady[1] and is never seen again. We are constantly made aware of Duncan's presence but only through the characters' elusive and contradictory accounts of him. When, in Act 1, Scene 7, Macbeth contemplates the murder of his king and rejects the thought with horror, his on-stage soliloquy is set off against Duncan's welcome banquet that is taking place off-stage. The banquet is indicated (as Shakespeare had done in *Romeo and Juliet* 1.4.) by the presence of servants: '*Enter a Sewer, and divers Servants with dishes and service ouer the stage.*' (1.7). In the earlier play, Shakespeare gave the servants some comic banter[2] but here their presence serves as a purely physical reminder of an alternative off-stage world of feasting and hospitality that frames Macbeth's planned treachery. We are reminded of this contrast between Duncan's world and Macbeth's immediately after Macbeth and his lady finally take the decision to kill their king. Banquo brings Macbeth a gift from the king, a reminder of the off-stage banquet and Macbeth's absence from it.

At the centre of the play another banquet is held, this time on stage. Macbeth calls together his thanes to celebrate his new power with a feast. On this occasion the off-stage world of murder intrudes with the arrival, first, of the murderer and then, disastrously, the ghost of the murdered Banquo. At the end of this banquet scene Macbeth remembers that Macduff is absent. His off-stage presence has not been noted before but the reminder of his existence begins the final action in which the witches' second prophecy triggers the violence against Macduff and his family.

18

After Duncan's murder, more of the violence takes place on stage. Banquo's death, which forms the second major movement of the play, is enacted in a scene that builds suspense as the murderers gather and question the mysterious third assassin. The actual killing is over in a moment, providing a brutal prelude to the gathering of the thanes at Macbeth's feast. The murderers, too, have come from a strange off-stage world that is barely incorporated into the on-stage action. Later, other unexplained murderers appear from off-stage to murder Macduff's family. The sense of gathering violence exists just out of sight and counterpoints Macbeth's and his lady's descent into desperation and madness.

This handling of on-stage and off-stage action, together with the changing rhythm of commentary and events, creates a powerful sense of the world of the play. It is a world that includes the possibility of points of view other than those of the main characters. At key moments, after Duncan's murder and between the banquet and Macbeth's return to the witches, there are extended commentary scenes (2.4 and 4.1.) in which generically named figures – an old man, an unidentified lord – offer guarded interpretations of events to Lennox, Ross and Macduff. They act as a reminder that Macbeth's attempts at control are under pressure from a human opposition and are not the subject merely of supernatural forces or the malign operations of the witches' prophecy.

Keeping the world off-stage is a powerful (and innovative) technical device that creates an intense focus on Macbeth and his lady. The presentation of these two characters is also unusual in that they are given nothing to do on stage. Their murder of the king takes place off-stage and the powerful symbolic role it has in the action is created entirely by the characters' language. The characters themselves seem to have an emotional life that existed before and goes beyond their roles in this particular action, but that effect too is generated entirely by the range of language that the writer gives them.

As we have seen, Macbeth's response to the witches in 1.3.126–40 introduces the language of ethical choice to the simple sequence of greetings offered him by the witches' prophecy. The force of his ethical choice, however, is given an added resonance by the way that those ethical questions are described in psychic and physical terms. Macbeth muses on the witches' prophecy in terms of its effect on both his body and his mind. The abstract 'supernatural soliciting' turns into a 'horrid image' that has the palpable physical effect that it 'doth unfix my hair/ And make my seated heart knock at my ribs,/ Against the use of nature'. Even the shifts in syntax are suggestive. Macbeth's line (1.3.148) 'My thought, whose murder yet is but fantastical,' leaves the reader (and viewer) unclear about the relationship between thought and fantasy and uncertain whether 'thought' is being murdered or is the idea of murder. The physical effects are perfectly clear but the thoughts that generate them are not.

The expression of Macbeth's confusion also has the effect of making the witches play a more complex role in the play's imaginary world. They move from being a narrative device, the bearers of messages, to becoming inextricably entangled in the representation of Macbeth's imagination and his bodily response to his unbidden thoughts.

This imaginative recreation of the witches' greeting continues in the letter that Macbeth's wife reads at the beginning of Act 1, Scene 5. In that letter, Macbeth changes the order of the events as they occur in the play. The letter recounts the proof ('the perfect'st report') of the witches' 'more than mortall knowledge' *before* it mentions the triple greeting that Macbeth has read as prophecy. This tiny change provides a different perspective on the events of the previous scenes. It puts Macbeth at the centre of the story and allows his wife to draw a conclusion about the future from his account of the past:

> Glamis thou art, and Cawdor, and shalt be
> What thou art promis'd;

> (1.5.13–14)

By this device of the letter, the witches become the connection between Macbeth's 'horrible imaginings' and his lady's more direct desire to

> chastise with the valour of my tongue
> All that impedes thee from the golden round,
> Which fate and metaphysical aid doth seem
> To have thee crowned withal.

> (1.5.24–7)

Macbeth's wife never sees the witches. However, by invoking 'the spirits that tend on mortal thoughts' she deepens the imaginative resonance of the play's supernatural ambiance. The action now takes place surrounded by a world where there are not only prophesying witches but also spirits who are invited literally to change Lady Macbeth's physical composition into one that will be fit for murder. She calls on them to

> Come you spirits,
> That tend on mortal thoughts, unsex me here,
> And fill me from the crown to the toe, top-full
> Of direst cruelty; make thick my blood,
> Stop up th'access, and passage to remorse,
> That no compunctious visitings of nature
> Shake my fell purpose nor keep peace between
> Th'effect and it. Come to my womans breasts,
> And take my milk for gall, you murd'ring ministers,
> Wherever in your sightless substances
> You wait on natures mischief

(1.5.38–48)

When Lady Macbeth asks the spirits to 'unsex' her, she is asking to be deprived of the attributes associated with her sex and the speech elaborates that process in detailed physiological terms. The spirits are to 'make thick my blood', making it flow less freely, less able to carry its purer parts to the brain. They will 'stop up the access and passage to remorse', preventing, in quite physical terms, the flow of female sympathies around her body. When they 'take my milk for gall' they will exchange the bodily fluids associated with compassion for the bile, secreted by the liver, that produces anger and bitterness. The milk that the lady wishes to be purged from her body is the same 'milk of human kindness' that she thinks will disable Macbeth's power 'to catch the nearest way' (1.5.15–16). The milk that fills Macbeth's body is the milk that he sucked from his mother; Lady Macbeth implies that it has not been transformed into the blood that would give him manly courage. This transformation of milk into blood is not merely physical; Lady Macbeth also associates it with 'human kindness'. Macbeth's bodily fluids, in his wife's view, will dispose him towards 'kindness', a term that includes 'kinship' with other humans.

21

None of this suggests that Lady Macbeth is a witch. The 'spirits' that she invokes are quite different from the witches' animal familiars, Paddock, the frog, and Graymalkin, the cat, that were associated with the superstitions of village witchcraft. Lady Macbeth's speech, by contrast, reflects the learned philosophical tradition in which magic and demonology were within a scientific spectrum that included physiology and medicine. As D.P. Walker explains 'The central permanent notion in all uses (of the word "spirit") is that of mediation between two extremes...angels as God's and demons as Satan's messengers and servants'.[3] So the spirits that Lady Macbeth invokes 'tend on mortal thoughts' as servants on their masters. The meaning of 'spirit' as an agent or a servant was extended to medical applications where the word referred to a corporeal vapour, centred in the brain and flowing through the nervous system: 'the first instrument of the incorporeal soul, an instrument for sense perception, imagination and motor activity – the link between body and soul'.[4]

The particular combination of biological and spiritual concepts used in Lady Macbeth's speech shows how the Renaissance model of human motivation included physical and ethical concepts that are, in modern usage, more often kept apart. However the speech was more than a passive re-iteration of received ideas. It shows an intense reworking of language – not least in making up the new word, 'unsex' – in order to communicate the depth of the transformation that Lady Macbeth associates with her preparation for murder.

That attention to language is also evident in the way that Lady Macbeth imagines a future action that she cannot acknowledge. She calls instead on the night to 'pall thee in the dunnest smoke of hell' (1.5.49). The night and not Lady Macbeth herself, will take on the purple colour of funeral vestments and thus associates the imagined action with death. The future action that she imagines will not be her own. She transposes the imagined action to a disembodied yet anthropomorphic 'keen knife' that cannot see the wound it makes and cannot be seen by heaven. The extraordinarily dense and convoluted language creates the psychological effect of a character who both embraces and displaces the action that is required for the fulfilment of the witches' prophecy.

Once Lady Macbeth has read her husband's letter, she never mentions the witches and their prophecy again. The act of murder itself is only ever referred to as a pronoun. Contemplating her husband's potential for action, Lady Macbeth says:

> What thou wouldst highly,
> That wouldst thou holily: wouldst not play false,
> And yet wouldst wrongly win. Thou'dst haue, great Glamis,
> That which cries, 'Thus thou must do', if thou have it;
> And that which rather thou dost fear to do,
> Than wishest should be undone.

> (1.5.18–23)

These lines are difficult to understand because Lady Macbeth does not state what the 'that' is that Macbeth 'wouldst have' (the crown) or the 'that' which he 'fears to do' (kill the king). The line could be glossed: 'You want to have that (the crown) which cries out "Thus thou must do" if you are to have it; And you want to do that (killing the king) which you are more afraid to do than you wish it not to be done'. The syntactic complexity of the lines creates a dramatic effect of an individual wrestling intellectually with knowledge of an evil deed that she resists and is intrigued by at one and the same time.

That knowledge of evil and good and the possibility of choice between them were both contained in the early-modern meaning of 'conscience', a much more active and theologically resonant concept then than it is now. It is echoed in Lady Macbeth's resistance to the 'compunctious visitings of nature'. The word 'compunctious', another Shakespeare coinage, literally meant 'pricking or puncturing' as a goad would be used to drive an ox. But this image of conscience is not only theological but is also associated with 'nature', the natural affinity with other human beings, invoked in the lady's reference to Macbeth's 'human kindness' (1.5.11). The concept of 'kindness' carries both the modern sense of sympathy for other human beings and an older sense of a distinct affinity with the human as opposed to animals (who are below humans) or spirits (who are above them).

The difficulties of this language are not merely those of older idioms or changing meanings of words. They constitute the dramatization of character, constructed out of a complex mix of theology, ethics and psychology rather than merely reflecting ordinary human behaviour. Similar complexities are similarly present in the 'conscience' speech that Macbeth delivers when he retreats from the banquet put on to welcome Duncan. He begins

> If it were done when 'tis done, then 'twere well
> It were done quickly: If th'assassination
> Could trammel up the consequence and catch
> With his surcease, success, that but this blow
> Might be the be-all, and the end-all – here,
> But here, upon this Banke and Shoal of time,
> We'd jump the life to come.

(1.7.1–7)

The linguistic complexity of these lines can be read merely as an image of Macbeth's tormented state of mind and that may be all that can be conveyed in performance. More importantly, however, they create a particular image of a troubled conscience: one that cannot speak of the contemplated deed, rather than one, as in *Hamlet* for example, whose every aspect is explored at length. The repeated 'it' of the opening line, requires the reader to collude with Macbeth in understanding the deed in question, and the repeated 'done' means something different in each reiteration: 'over and done with', 'enacted', 'acted upon'. The parenthetic clauses and repeated starts in the second sentence require the reader's total attention to understand what is being proposed. The use of unusual words such as 'surcease', a legal term, meaning a stay of proceedings, both distances the brutal reality of murder and, through the alliteration with 'success', elides the relationship between the act and its consequences. The contorted language of the first few lines are then resolved with a sense of relief in the active, monosyllabic familiarity of the verb in 'we'd *jump* the life to come'. The lines gain their effect from the fact that behind the difficult language is a vivid and simple physical image of a man leaping across a stream. By invoking the commonplace metaphor of the 'river of time' but transposing it to 'this bank and shoal of time' these lines reinvigorate the cliché and produce the powerful imaginative connection between the speech and Macbeth's situation.

These opening lines dramatize Macbeth's struggle to imagine Duncan's murder being done without seeing himself doing it.

He escapes into metaphor in order to avoid contemplating the possibility of his own action. He is, of course, fully aware, in general terms, of his wider political and ethical relationships. He remembers that Duncan, his king, is 'here in double trust':

> He's here in double trust:
> First, as I am his kinsman, and his subject,
> Strong both against the deed: Then, as his host,
> Who should against his murderer shut the door,
> Not bear the knife my self.

(1.7.12–16)

He then imagines the consequences of the deed, not in physical danger to himself, but in the protesting clamour of cosmic forces, disturbed by the violent action:

> his virtues
> Will plead like angels, trumpet-tongued against
> The deep damnation of his taking-off:
> And pity, like a naked new-born babe,
> Striding the blast, or heaven's cherubin, horsed
> Upon the sightless couriers of the air,
> Shall blow the horrid deed in every eye,
> That tears shall drown the wind.

(1.7.18–25)

The poetic rendering of Macbeth's terror produces an apocalyptic image of the whole sky filled with angels and cherubim marshalled to denounce him and his 'horrid deed': the unmentionable murder of a king.

The whole passage is a single clause describing the action of Duncan's virtues that are personified as a supplicant pleading against damnation in heaven's court. However, the phrase 'deep damnation' intensified by the alliteration does double duty since Duncan's 'taking off', his death, does not damn Duncan but Macbeth. The difficulty of understanding the passage comes from the peculiar effect of compression. It confuses Duncan's damnation with Macbeth's, and it extends the similes so that they lose connection with their originating concepts.

The image of the angels pleading then generates the further, syntactically complicated, passage describing the action of 'pity'. Pity is personified as 'a naked new born babe' but the action of this personified figure is itself difficult to understand because of

25

the linguistic leaps of the passage: 'Pity...shall blow the horrid deed in every eye'. The general sense is clear – pity will reveal the horrid deed. However, 'blow in every eye' is an unusual image for revelation. The verb 'blow' is perhaps suggested by the angels' trumpets. What is curious is that it will be blown in every eye rather than in every *ear*. 'Eye' could have arisen from the idea of the 'sightless couriers' that are, like the 'sightless substances' invoked by Lady Macbeth, both invisible and blind. This image of sightlessness with its connection to eyes leads onto the further image of 'tears shall drown the wind', itself a complex idea. The wind connects back to 'the blast' stridden by the naked new-born babe but the notion of tears drowning the wind can be both a commonplace connection between rain and wind and the idea that an object blown into the eye will make it fill with tears.

The passage is extended by the additional simile comparing pity with 'heaven's cherubim, horsed/Upon the sightless couriers of the air'. A noun, 'horse', is turned into a passive verb 'horsed', meaning 'on horseback'. The image possibly derived from the baby angels that decorated the borders of woodcuts on religious themes.[5] It also connects back to the four horsemen of the apocalypse, the personifications of pestilence, fire, famine and war. But these connections are never made explicit: the cherubim are riding, not on horseback but on 'the sightless couriers of the air', yet another metaphor for the wind. The two similes for pity – as a naked new born babe *and* as heaven's cherubim – suggest a contradiction in which pity is both weak and helpless and yet strong enough to carry the power of divine revelation and divine retribution.

These two great 'conscience' speeches from Macbeth and his lady use complex poetry to extend the ethical and psychic ranges of the characters who deliver them. They situate the characters in a universe that includes angels and spirits and in which the shared and understood, but unspoken, action of murder will resonate far beyond its immediate consequences.

In spite of the ethical and theological complexity of these ideas the play does not leave these characters in the realm of ethical abstraction. It also brings them together and out of their brief lines of dialogue creates a sense of a powerful personal relationship that spills beyond the boundaries of its action. From their first meeting in Act 1, Scene 5, Lady Macbeth is bent on action:

> He that's coming,
> Must be provided for, and you shall put
> This night's great business into my dispatch
>
> (1.5.64–6)

When the couple next meet, in Act 1, Scene 7, she remains entirely focused on the forward movement from desire to action. She dismisses Macbeth's pangs of conscience as a moral hangover:

> Was the hope drunk
> Wherein you dressed your self? Hath it slept since?
> And wakes it now to look so green and pale
> At what it did so freely?
>
> (1.7.34–7)

His eloquent contemplation of the consequences of his imagined act are reduced to

> Letting I dare not, wait upon I would,
> Like the poor cat i'th' adage.
>
> (1.7.43–4)

The language of their exchange extends the simple opposition between a contemplative Macbeth and his active lady. Lady Macbeth's humiliating images of Macbeth's weakness shift the conversation to question how men and women behave. Macbeth tries to stem the flow of his lady's contempt by asserting

> I dare do all that may become a man,
> Who dares do more, is none
>
> (1.7.46–7)

Editors since Rowe in the eighteenth century have tried to give a more complex resonance to these lines by changing the 'dares *no* more' printed in the Folio text to 'dares *do* more'. The revised version suggests a fine distinction between ordinary manly behaviour and behaviour, such as killing a king, that is unbecoming to a man and therefore not manly at all. The Folio text's version, however, does not offer this complexity and leaves the second line simply glossing the first. At this stage, the contrast is not between men and women's behaviour but between the actions of men (who are capable of contemplation) and beasts who act merely on impulse. Lady Macbeth, however, refuses the conventional comparison. She asks

> What beast was't then
> That made you break this enterprise to me?
> When you durst do it, then you were a man:
> And to be more than what you were, you would
> Be so much more the man.

(1.7.47–51)

Her lines identify a more extended hierarchy going from 'beast' to 'man' (one capable of doing that he dares) and the unmentionable 'more than what you were', a king. She then adds the extraordinary assertion about her own capacity for completing the movement from promise to action:

> I haue given suck, and know
> How tender 'tis to love the babe that milks me:
> I would, while it was smiling in my face,
> Have plucked my nipple from his boneless gums,
> And dashed the brains out, had I so sworn
> As you have done to this.

(1.7.54–9)

The physical precision of these lines, their parallel active verbs (plucked and dashed) raises the stakes of the discussion. Lady Macbeth is not discussing the abstract qualities of manhood but focusing brutally on violent action. She articulates exactly what kind of action is required and explains her plan to her husband. Macbeth's delighted response returns to the question of manliness and femininity:

> Bring forth men-children only,
> For thy undaunted mettle should compose
> Nothing but males.

(1.7.72–4)

Lady Macbeth's 'mettle', the physical composition that, according to early-modern physiology, provided the substance for new birth, is suited to the production of male children but the punning echoes of mettle and metal and male and mail (as in armour) also create a shadowy image of a man in battle, the role in which Macbeth has been most successful at the beginning of the play.

The dense linguistic resonances of this scene extend it well beyond a banal sexual contest. The scene presents Macbeth's lady goading her husband to commit the act that will fulfil the witches' prophecy. The psychic and rhetorical resources that she is given to do so, allow the scene to open up larger questions about the differences between men and beasts as well as between women and men. The couple's desire to murder their king is thus defined not only in terms of the characters' individual desires but in a realm of inhuman behaviour that makes the lady imagine the most unwomanly act of infanticide as a corollary to her husband's unmanly and beast-like cowardice.

When next we see Macbeth and his lady together, the murder is done. Since the deed itself takes place off-stage, full attention can be paid to the couple's reaction to it. Their psychic trauma is dramatized in the broken verse lines and the oscillation between Macbeth's frantic recollection and his lady's anxious efforts to calm him. When they first meet, a single blank-verse line is broken into single word exchanges:

LADY. Did not you speak?
MACBETH.   When?
LADY.   Now.
MACBETH.   As I descended?

(2.2.16–19)

The firm framework of the blank verse line holds the exchange together but the single words keep the two speakers apart, both psychically and linguistically. It is a technically brilliant device that shows the writer resisting the obvious rhetorical tropes of extreme emotion in favour of a pared down, unspoken, representation of the couple's reaction.[6] When Macbeth's speech does move into more expansive description of the murder scene, he turns away from the image of the murdered Duncan to an almost obsessive attention to the sleeping grooms:

There's one did laugh in's sleep, and one cried 'Murder',
That they did wake each other; I stood, and heard them,
But they did say their prayers, And addressed them
Again to sleep
.   .   .   .   .
One cried 'God bless us!' and 'Amen' the other,
As they had seen me with these hangman's hands.

29

List'ning their fear, I could not say 'Amen',
When they did say 'God bless us'.

(2.2.24–32)

Macbeth's focus on the grooms is unexpected and so creates a
sense of psychological idiosyncracy, a sense of an individual
responding spontaneously to real events.

After the murder, the division of speeches reverses Macbeth's
and his lady's earlier discussion of the planned murder in Act 1,
Scene 7. There the lady had the long speeches and Macbeth the
short interventions. This time, her attempts to calm him come in
single sentences that barely disrupt his frantic recollection of the
spectacle of Duncan's death. When he embarks on a raving
excursus on the nature of sleep, she interrupts him with a
puzzled 'what do you mean?' and when he imagines the cry of
'sleep no more', she asks 'Who was it that thus cried?' Her
practical focus on the here and now, her refusal imaginatively to
contemplate the deed's implications, widens the gap between
her and her husband.

This differentiation between Macbeth's agonized contemplation of his action and the lady's practical courage reverses the
usual gendered division between active men and contemplative
women. It is given a theatrical resonance in the treatment of the
bloody daggers that Macbeth brings from the murder scene. The
daggers are not revealed for some 40 lines after Macbeth's
entrance. When Lady Macbeth sees them, her angry question –
'why did you bring these daggers from the place?' – breaks
across her efforts to soothe her husband. The physicality of the
bloody daggers, their position between Macbeth and his lady
draws an audience's eyes to them, creating an emblematic
tableau that has been reproduced in illustrations throughout the
play's performance history.

The lady's reaction is one of impatient practicality: 'Infirm of
purpose/Give me the daggers'. She goes on to insist that

The sleeping and the dead
Are but as pictures: 'tis the eye of child-hood,
That fears a painted devil.

(2.2.56–8)

She dismisses the supernatural and Macbeth's imaginative
response to it as belonging to the realm of children. She does

the same, later in the play, when she rejects Macbeth's terror at Banquo's ghost as no more than 'A woman's story at a winter's fire,/authorised by her grandam' (3.4.65–6). Her scepticism about the world of the imaginary and the supernatural is at odds with her earlier appeal to 'the spirits that tend on mortal thought'. After the murder, her views are closer to those of learned men who were at pains to associate spirits and ghosts with the low culture of women and children.[7]

The bloody daggers create a physical connection between the scene on stage and the off-stage scene of Duncan's murder. Macbeth and his lady react to them in different ways that begin to drive a wedge between them. For Lady Macbeth the misplaced daggers present a practical problem and the impact of the blood that so appals Macbeth can be distanced by a punning joke. As she returns to the scene of Duncan's murder she says

> If he do bleed,
> I'll gild the faces of the grooms withal,
> For it must seem their guilt.
>
> (2.2.58–60)

Once the first realization of murder is over, Macbeth can echo his lady's wordplay on 'guilt' and 'gilt' in his rhetorical reaction to the public revelation of Duncan's death. He excuses his intemperate act in killing the grooms with a much more controlled presentation of the scene than the one with which he greeted his lady:

> Here lay Duncan.
> His silver skin, laced with his golden blood
> And his gashed stabs, looked like a breach in nature,
> For ruin's wasteful entrance. There the murderers,
> Steeped in the colours of their trade; their daggers
> Unmannerly breeched with gore. Who could refrain,
> That had a heart to love and in that heart,
> Courage to make's love known?
>
> (2.3.104–11)

Macbeth's account of the murder scene is presented to the audience on stage in ways that suggest a controlled and authoritative description. The murder scene itself does not appear on stage and so it can be conjured up in two quite different ways. It exists only in the imaginary off-stage world and so can be subject to different forms of representation for different purposes.

The physical representation of the daggers after the murder indicate the ways in which Shakespeare manages the connection between the physical dimension of the stage and the characters' language. The daggers, in effect, stand in for the off-stage murder and they also re-present the disembodied dagger that haunted Macbeth as he made his way to kill his king.

When Lady Macbeth scolds her husband for his terror at Banquo's ghost, she explicitly connects it to the appearance of that 'air-drawn dagger'. There is no scene where he has told her of his vision, but the reader has experienced it with Macbeth and it is part of the accumulation of theatrical images that accompany the play's narrative and give the reader and viewer the powerful sense of a complete world in which this action takes place.

In the scene where Macbeth sees the spectral dagger, the audience's attention is drawn by the interrogative in Macbeth's opening lines: 'Is this a dagger which I see before me, /The handle toward my hand?' (2.1.33-4). In modern performance it is hard to avoid spooky melodrama but the Folio text uses the episode to explore the relationship between sensory perception and psychic state which is such an important part of the way that character is created. Macbeth's lines explore that relationship quite explicitly:

> Art thou not, fatal vision, sensible
> To feeling, as to sight? Or art thou but
> A dagger of the mind, a false creation,
> Proceeding from the heat-oppressed brain?

> (2.1.36–9)

The connection between psychic reality and the palpable, material world is then insisted on as Macbeth draws his own dagger. He still sees the spectral dagger, but concludes that it emanates from his own consciousness:

> There's no such thing:
> It is the bloody business, which informs
> Thus to mine eyes.

> (2.1.47–9)

He leaves the stage carrying one dagger and when next we see him, that dagger, and another, are, like the air-drawn dagger, covered in blood. A powerful connection is thus established between Macbeth's imagination of 'the bloody business' before the act, his broken reaction after he has done the deed, when blood is imagined as all-engulfing, making even the ocean 'one red', and his later, more controlled, presentation of the tableau of the murdered Duncan and his grooms.

For Lady Macbeth, the psychic movement between imagined horror and material reality flows in the opposite direction. She begins with a practical, almost domestic, reaction to the problems of blood and daggers: 'a little water clears us of this deed'. She never sees Banquo's ghost and manages the thane's departure from the disrupted banquet.

Lady Macbeth is given only a brief and poignant speech to indicate her disappointment at the failure of her plans:

> Nought's had, all's spent,
> Where our desire is got without content:
> 'Tis safer, to be that which we destroy,
> Than by destruction dwell in doubtful joy.

(3.2.4–7)

The directness of this language provides one of the play's most succinct images of the devastating gap between aspiration and achievement. The rhymes (spent/content; destroy/joy) connect the opposing elements but the lady is given no more eloquent elaboration of her regret or imaginative analysis of her situation. Her advice to Macbeth sums up her approach: 'Things without all remedy/Should be without regard; what's done is done' (3.2. 11–1.2). The echo of the opening line of Macbeth's conscience speech in 1.7 resonates and foreshadows her collapse in the sleep-walking scene that suggests the psychic cost of her controlled reaction to events.

The linguistic particularity of Lady Macbeth's speeches allows an idiosyncratic character to be created out of a figure who appears in less than half of the scenes in the play. The key images of her speeches recur through the play, binding together the language and the action into a totality that suggests a human being who has experienced a trauma that recurs through obsessive repetition. Though she appears in few scenes, her passing references to the events that Macbeth has experienced create the illusion of her off-stage life with him. She knows about the 'air-drawn dagger'; she attempts to stand between Macbeth and his bewildered thanes when he sees Banquo's ghost and, most critically, in the sleep-walking scene, she knows that Macduff's wife and children have been murdered.

The sleep-walking scene, critically positioned before the final conflict between Macbeth and the English forces, summarizes the key events of the play through the distorted, unconnected images of her speech. The spots of blood that she tries to rub from her hands are an ironic reminder of her earlier certainty that 'A little water clears us of this deed' (2.2) and her astonishment that 'the old man would have had so much blood in him' (5.1.33–4) counterpoints the punning mockery of her earlier plan to 'gild the faces of the grooms withal' (2.2.59).

Behind each fractured image of the sleep-walking speech, there lies an image of a relationship in which she has desperately tried to prevent her husband from revealing their deadly secret: 'No more o' that, my lord, no more o' that. You mar all with this starting' (5.1.37–8). The lines, 'Wash your hands, put on your nightgown, look not so pale' (5.1.52–3) brings a vivid reminder of their reaction to the knocking that brings Duncan's thanes onto the stage of murder. Her reassurance 'I tell you yet again, Banquo's buried; he cannot come out on's grave' (5.1.52–3) offers a fleeting image of a scene that does not take place in the play but serves fully to realize the imagined world of the couple's psychic collapse. The sleep-walking scene prepares the audience for Macbeth's despair at his wife's death and the desperate resolution of the finale. The whole sequence of Duncan's murder from Macbeth's wish that 'If it were done, when 'tis done, 'twere best it were done quickly' (1.7.1–2) to their panicked moment after the murder, is summed up in 'To bed, to bed; there's knocking at the gate. Come, come, come, come, give me your hand; what's done cannot be undone. To bed, to bed, to bed' (5.1.56–8).

Each sentence of the sleep-walking scene is a reminder of a discrete event in the previous action. Together they enact an obsessive return of repressed memory in a scene which has defined a psychic state for subsequent representations of obsessive mental illness. The scene also offers a brilliant dramatic summary of the events that have created the situation of the play's approaching finale. The sleep-walking scene stands between the events in England where Macduff joins the English forces and their first arrival in Scotland. The eerie night-time revelation of the lady's passion opens into the calm battle-preparations of Menteith, Angus and Caithness, figures who have had no part in the action of murder. The remainder of the play will open out the action from its intense focus on the main characters. Its final resolution comes from Macduff and the English forces, figures whose roles in the play come from beyond the closed world of Macbeth and his lady.

3

Working with Ideas

The characters of Macbeth and his lady are so powerfully realized that they tend to dominate readings of the play. However, the work's overall structure juxtaposes their view of events with other perspectives that provide a sounding board for hearing the resonant significance of their tragedy. One of the key points of reference for those wider debates is the figure of Banquo. He is a shadowy presence in the play's action and is dead by the end of Act 3, but he looms large in Macbeth's eloquent imagination and his presence as a ghost. He is the focal point of the procession of kings and this gives him even greater theatrical power dead than alive.

As we have seen, the witches' prophecy refers not only to Macbeth's future as king but also to Banquo:

> FIRST WITCH. Lesser than Macbeth and greater.
> SECOND WITCH. Not so happy, yet much happier.
> THIRD WITCH. Thou shalt get kings, though thou be none.
> So all hail Macbeth, and Banquo.
> FIRST WITCH. Banquo, and Macbeth, all hail.
>
> (1.3.63–7)

The play gives Banquo scant opportunity to develop his thoughts on the implications of the witches' message. On the night of Macbeth's banquet to welcome Duncan, he briefly suggests that he fears the dreams that sleep will bring:

> A heavy summons lies like lead upon me,
> And yet I would not sleep; merciful powers,
> Restrain in me the cursed thoughts that nature
> Gives way to in repose.
>
> (2.1.6–9)

Here Banquo is briefly presented as a figure moved by the witches' revelation but he is not given the complex of theatrical images, poetic elaborations and narrative events that, as we have seen, create character for Macbeth and his lady. His brief but suggestive speech about the effect the witches have had on him opens out the possibility of speculation about Banquo's motives and character: is his ambition as great as Macbeth's? How might he have dealt with power? It demonstrates, once again, the play's ability to spin off other stories and give tantalizing glimpses of a creative space in which the play might have had different emphases, or in which the contrast and conflict between Macbeth and Banquo fuelled the main narrative. In this play, however, Banquo's role is to extend the action beyond the king killing, to create a new objective for Macbeth's action after Duncan is dead while at the same time offering a view into an alternative way of dealing with the structures of power in the world of Duncan and his thanes. By making Banquo the father of kings, the work addresses kingship as a system in time that goes beyond personal power.

The particular complex of ideas that surrounded 'kingship' in the early modern period may be difficult for a modern reader or audience to understand. Kingship as a psychic, political and intellectual reality is one of the casualties of modernity. Ideas about kingship have been seen as a set of beliefs locked in the past. They have been relegated to footnotes that explain a closed system in which the continuity of a symbolic kingship, ordained by God, transcended the mortal being that held the office at any given time. As a result, Macbeth's and his lady's passionate reaching for 'the golden round' is sometimes read as a study in more generic, abstract aspiration such as 'ambition' or, more recently, 'authority and power'.[1] Banquo's role, however, both as a character and in the narrative, is one means by which this play negotiates its way through ideas about kingship that were changing in Shakespeare's time. The play turns these contested and changing ideas into dramatic events and key physical images in order to contribute to the story-telling and emotional drive of the whole action.

Banquo's presence in the first encounter with the witches allows the play to offer the intriguing possibility of a response to their greeting which is different from Macbeth's. It goes on to show how that difference arises from a different relationship to King Duncan. When Banquo and Macbeth greet the king in 1.4. after the witches' revelations, the king welcomes Macbeth in formal speech:

> O worthiest cousin,
> The sin of my ingratitude even now
> Was heavy on me. Thou art so far before,
> That swiftest wing of recompense is slow,
> To overtake thee. Would thou hadst less deserved,
> That the proportion both of thanks and payment,
> Might have been mine: only I have left to say,
> More is thy due than more than all can pay.
>
> (1.4.14–21)

The elegant convolutions of Duncan's language make the formal statement that Macbeth's actions have exceeded the king's ability to reward them. These ideas, however, are not just the opinions of an individual character. They draw on long-standing ideas about the importance of reciprocity in which the balance of favours and obligations must be evenly distributed and a surplus of obligation is as undesirable as a surplus of debt. Macbeth, equally formally, insists that he is doing no more than he should, since his service to the king is built into and secures a relationship in which each person plays their allotted role:

> Your highness' part,
> Is to receive our duties, and our duties
> Are to your throne, and state, children, and servants,
> Which do but what they should, by doing everything
> Safe toward your love and honour.
>
> (1.4.23–7)

There need be nothing sinister in this exchange of formalities.[2] Nevertheless, it is very different from the physical gesture that accompanies the king's greeting to Banquo: 'Let me enfold thee,/And hold thee to my heart' (1.4.31–2), an embrace accompanied by tears of joy. The contrast between Duncan's welcome to the two thanes is a tiny stage moment, possibly forgotten in the important exchange when Duncan names Malcolm as his heir. However, it is reinforced (and can be emphasized in performance) by Banquo's subsequent actions in bringing Macbeth the king's gift of a diamond in the scene immediately after Macbeth and his lady have resolved to commit the murder. In the culture of reciprocity indicated by the king's earlier speeches, a gift is of more than monetary value. It signals and seals the relationship of service between king and thane. After Banquo has delivered the king's gift to Macbeth, he raises the question of 'the three weird sisters'. He is fobbed off by Macbeth's claim that 'I think not of them' (2.1.21) but Macbeth nonetheless begins his attempt to ensure Banquo's support, hinting that it might be rewarded by 'honour'.

Macbeth uses 'honour' to mean 'reward', as he does when he protests to his lady that Duncan 'hath honoured me of late' (1.7.32). Banquo's response, however, shows that honour can be seen as a more absolute virtue:

> So I lose none,
> In seeking to augment it, but still keep
> My bosom franchised, and allegiance clear,
> I shall be counselled.
>
> (2.1.26–9)

Banquo is being presented as a thane whose language and actions position him clearly in the culture of reciprocity where the thanes' first duty is to their king and when that duty is fulfilled, it is rewarded by the king's protection and largesse. The basis for these relationships is less a matter of personal commitment than a sense of comfort in a situation that is stable and clearly understood. That comfort is, of course, severely shaken by the king's death. After the murder, Banquo refers to 'our naked frailties' and the higher allegiance to 'the great hand of God' in which the thanes must fight against 'undivulged pretence ... of treasonous malice' (2.3.122–4).

After Duncan's murder, when there is no longer any clear source of kingly authority there are new opportunities for Banquo. He does speculate, in his only soliloquy, about the possible truth of the witches' prophecy:

> If there come truth from them,
> As upon thee, Macbeth, their speeches shine,
> Why by the verities on thee made good,
> May they not be my oracles as well,
> And set me up in hope.
>
> (3.1.6–10)

39

Like Macbeth, Banquo is shown to be aware of the connection between one prophetic truth and another. The play, however, gives no further dramatic space to Banquo's hopes and fears. His speech is interrupted by the arrival of Macbeth and his retinue. The dramatic dynamic created by Macbeth's interruption of Banquo's soliloquy creates a contrast between his future hopes and the physical and immediate reality of Macbeth's power represented in the extensive retinue that crowds onto the stage.

> *Sennet sounded. Enter* MACBETH *as King,* LADY MACBETH *as Queen* LENNOX, ROSS, *Lords and Attendants.*

(3.1.10)

From this point on, the staging of the play pushes Banquo from the centre stage and focuses attention on the contrast between Macbeth's power, represented by a collection of followers, and his psychic anxiety that takes place around the edges of the public scenes. Macbeth is represented, in the words of the stage direction '*as King*' but the kind of king that he will become is treated in soliloquy and in secret.

Banquo's presence permeates this section of the play but more attention is given to Macbeth's anxiety about Banquo than the figure of Banquo himself. After his first '*as King*' entrance, Macbeth invites Banquo to his feast and immediately summons the murderers. There follows the soliloquy in which he articulates at length the particular reproach that Banquo offers to his authority as king:

> Our fears in Banquo
> Stick deep, and in his royalty of nature
> Reigns that which would be feared. 'Tis much he dares,
> And to that dauntless temper of his mind,
> He hath a wisdom, that doth guide his valour,
> To act in safety. There is none but he,
> Whose being I doe fear; and under him,
> My genius is rebuk'd, as it is said
> Mark Antony's was by Cæsar.

(3.1.50–8)

There has been no time to demonstrate Banquo's possession of these qualities in the play. They exist as part of the obsessive fantasy with which Macbeth's speeches articulate both his own desires and their ethical opposite.

The contrast that Macbeth's speech articulates is not a simple one between good and evil. Its complex language is working out ideas about the nature of kingly and manly virtue that have a particular purchase in Renaissance psychology and physiology. The 'dauntless temper' of Banquo's mind is a phrase invented by Shakespeare that includes the idea of fearlessness and the physical process of 'tempering' or hardening steel. The whole passage describes the 'temperate' personality who balances courage with wisdom. There is an echo there of Lady Macbeth's taunt that Macbeth was 'afeard/To be the same in thine own act, and valour,/As thou art in desire' (1.7.40–1) which suggests that Shakespeare may have been circling round these ideas of the right behaviour for a man as well as putting together the dramatization of a mighty conflict between Macbeth and Banquo. The language continuously connects Macbeth's complaint with his own reflections on the rewards for treachery. Banquo's power to produce a future generation of kings poisons Macbeth's pleasure in his own kingship:

> For Banquo's issue have I filed my minde;
> For them, the gracious Duncan have I murdered,
> Put rancours in the vessel of my peace
> Only for them, and mine eternal jewel
> Given to the common enemy of man,
> To make them kings, the seeds of Banquo kings.

(3.1.66–71)

The idea that Banquo has 'put rancours (bitterness) in the vessel of my peace' is a reminder of the 'poisoned chalice' (1.7.11) that Macbeth had earlier imagined as the outcome of Duncan's murder and the 'eternal jewel' that he has given to the 'common enemy of man', the devil, recalls the diamond that Duncan had sent to Macbeth's wife after the banquet.

This speech is particularly effectively placed in the narrative. It follows on from Macbeth's first entrance 'as King' with his panoply of lords and attendants and it precedes his first act as king which is to plot Banquo's death. The conspiracy against Banquo is necessary for the continuing action even though it makes no sense in narrative time. The off-stage time when Macbeth might have met the murderers and spoken with them about their alleged grudge against Banquo is left unexplored since the murderers have a single, instrumental role to fulfil. The encounter with them, especially as Macbeth's first act as king, dramatizes the conniving and treachery necessary to sustain illegitimate kingship and it has resonances that continue throughout the play.

The scene with the murderers presents Macbeth as a competent, if immoral, tyrant. It is a rare moment in which the tactical demands of kingship are dramatized since the play, for the most part, puts the strictly political implications of the action in second place to the ethical and the psychic. Macbeth's rage at the witches' spoiling prophecy to Banquo presents an imaginative rather than an analytical account of political process:

> Upon my head they placed a fruitless crown,
> And put a barren scepter in my gripe,
> Thence to be wrenched with an unlineal hand,
> No son of mine succeeding.

(3.1.62–5)

There are, nonetheless, larger political implications for the view of kingship that the play presents. The list of adjectives in this speech – fruitless, barren, unlineal – emphasizes a view of kingship that sees it less as an office and more as a process of inheritance, the natural progression from father to son. Historically and in practice, of course, that progression was neither smooth nor universally accepted[3] but the play's events and its dramatic structure insist on the validity of that patrilineal model. Duncan's announcement of Malcolm's succession triggers the action of the play and the play's finale assures Malcolm's succession and gives due place to any opposition by the creation of the earls. The play translates the political idea about the legitimacy of succession into theatrical and narrative terms.

After the murder, Macbeth attempts to seal his kingship with a further feast. The feast is, of course, poisoned by the murder of Banquo whose ghostly presence disrupts the harmony of the ceremonial occasion. As Lady Macbeth reminds Macbeth when he is distracted by the appearance of the first murderer, a king's feast is more than the mere consumption of food. As Lady Macbeth insists, when Macbeth's attention is taken by the arrival of the first murderer:

42

> the feast is sold
> That is not often vouched, while 'tis a making,
> 'Tis given with welcome. To feed were best at home:
> From thence, the sauce to meat is ceremony,
> Meeting were bare without it.
>
> (3.4.33–7)

And when she fails to calm Macbeth's hysterical response to the ghost, his wife chides him with

> You have displaced the mirth,
> Broke the good meeting, with most admired disorder.
>
> (3.4.109–10)

Duncan's murder has created a catastrophic rupture in the cycle of obligation that could have linked the king and his subjects. Macbeth's actions as king show the conflict between his individualist will to power and his deep desire for those social relations between the king and his thanes, symbolized by feasting.

These familiar relations of gifts and feasting are presented in the play as the necessary ceremonies which protect the culture from atavistic violence. Macbeth's reaction to Banquo's ghost is not just personal fear but an awareness of a deeper sense that this is an apparition that threatens the very foundations of his culture:

> If charnel-houses, and our graves must send
> Those that we bury back, our monuments
> Shall be the maws of kites.
>
> (3.4.71–3)

Macbeth's offence in killing both Banquo and the king is not merely the sin of murder but a disruption of the civilizing ties which keep his social world in one piece. It returns Scotland to the lawless 'olden time / Ere humane statute purged the gentle weal' (3.4.75–6).

The feast in 3.4 is a pivotal moment in the play. It fills the stage, it includes the physical excitement of the appearance of Banquo's ghost and the disordered departure of the thanes and it provides the turning point in the narrative when Macbeth realizes that the supernatural forces that surround him are beyond his control.

Macbeth's disruption of the rightful connection between kingship and an ancient social world is reiterated in the discussion between Lennox and an anonymous lord (3.6). This conversation takes place in the hiatus between Macbeth's decision to return to the sisters (3.4.136–7) and the presentation of the prophetic apparitions.

The exchange between Lennox and the lord is a masterpiece of understatement and ambiguity. Lennox carefully puts the most positive gloss on the Macbeth's summary action against the grooms of Duncan's bedchamber. His assertion that Macbeth 'has borne all things well' is, of course, deeply ironic. Nevertheless it does not deny a king's right to exercise summary judgement and the rest of the speech focuses on the primary relationship of father and son and the rights of revenge rather than the more institutional requirements of kingship. The lord's response is less circumspect. He calls Macbeth 'this tyrant' and tells of Malcolm's plan to solicit aid from England. The desired outcome of Malcolm's diplomatic endeavours, moreover, is once again described in terms of social and ethical relations rather than explicitly political ones. The lord hopes that, with God's help

> we may again
> Give to our tables meat, sleep to our nights,
> Free from our feasts, and banquets bloody knives,
> Do faithful homage, and receive free honours,
> All which we pine for now.

> (3.6. 33–7)

There is no suggestion that Malcolm's return will necessarily produce a change in political or legal structures, merely that it will fulfil the deep desire for peace and the social harmony which is ensured by the familiar cycle of homage and honour, initiated in Duncan's welcome to Macbeth in Act 1 and sealed by harmonious feasting.

This dramatic transformation of ancient political ideas into the emotional fabric of the play is one of the great achievements of this work. It reaches a climax in the witches' final scene. There, the presentation of the show of kings is a ghastly reversal of the formal shows that were regularly presented for monarchs all over Europe. Those presentations endorsed and legitimated the position of the monarch and this show reverses their political message by presenting a procession in time that indicates the succession of kings without any reference to the political procedures which structure and legitimate that succession. The procession, like time itself, cannot be stopped by Macbeth's rage as it stretches out to the crack of doom. But the dramatic connection between that movement of time and the particular moment in this play's narrative is created by the final tableau that links Macbeth back to Banquo:

> Now I see 'tis true,
> For the blood-boltered Banquo smiles upon me,
> And points at them for his.

(4.1.121–3)

This is Banquo's final appearance, the play's third movement, and the discussion of kingship moves away from the ancient relation between king and thane. In turning to the invasion of Scotland by the English forces, it moves into the different political territory of resistance to violent usurpation. Malcolm's right to the Scottish throne had been established early in the play when Duncan announced his succession. This announcement triggered Macbeth's realization that the witches' prophecy would not be fulfilled by chance. It is, he says 'a step, /On which I must fall down, or else o're-leap' (1.4.48–9) but this specifically political question (as against the ethical questions of murder of a kinsman) is pushed into the background until the play's final sequence that presents the political solution in a new kind of kingship, a coalition between the English and the Scots.

The final scenes that feature the English-backed invasion present a familiar image of historical relations between the English and the Scots which were characterized by the invasion of Scottish territories by border magnates, acting in the name of the English king and with the connivance of Scottish aspirants to the throne. Historical accuracy, however, is less significant than the way that these scenes dramatize Malcolm's legitimacy as king through his leadership of the invading army and his ability to draw to him the support of Siward's forces. At the end of the play, Malcolm makes a significant conciliatory political gesture. He disperses his power and shares it with the Scottish thanes. He declares that his thanes and kinsmen should 'Henceforth be earls, the first that ever Scotland/ In such an honour named' (5.9.29–30). In returning peace to Scotland, Malcolm also ensured its continuity by establishing a new category of nobleman, an honour familiar to the English. The primitive and unstable rule of Scotland is reformed by English honours. Malcolm's creation of the loyal thanes as 'earls' may have had a special resonance at the time when James was attempting to create a 'union of nobility' by giving titles to both English and Scots gentry as a way of binding their allegiance both to him personally and to the United Kingdom.[4]

Malcolm's political legitimacy is not merely a matter of historical accuracy, however. Its dramatic presentation is an important part of the effect of the play's finale and it holds out the possibility of a new, modern, kind of kingship that will resolve the conflict of times past.[5] The politics of this last part of the play, however, are less securely presented in dramatic terms. There is less dramatic space to develop Malcolm's role as a legitimate king and the emotional force of resistance to Macbeth is divided between Banquo and Macduff. Duncan's sons are presented as completely cowed by the events surrounding their father's death and, after his father's murder, Malcolm disappears from the stage until the curious scene in the English court where he encounters Macduff. Malcolm's unwillingness to accept Macduff's allegiance and his question about why Macduff has left his children behind in Scotland both reveal the need for political opposition to be dramatically legitimated by an experience of personal and familial loss.

The set piece account of the English king Edward's magical powers of healing (4.3.146–59) and the strange extended dialogue in which Malcolm pretends to be an entirely unsuitable king in order to test Macduff, both dramatize the uneasy tension that permeates political exile and also reveal the gap between a political and a dramatic presentation of the issues. Malcolm and Macduff's debate over the nature of 'king-becoming graces' is precisely focused in early modern political theory but sits less firmly in the play's structure of feeling. The debate defines an appropriate balance between the personal virtue of a king and his right to succeed, giving striking emphasis to Malcolm's role as peace-maker, responsible for the good conduct of his country. It insists on the political role of the king as more significant than the personal relations with particular subjects and in doing so, reinforces an idea of kingship that depends more on political legitimacy ensured by lineage than on the personal qualities or the nature of the individual who happens to hold the office at the time. In Malcolm's case the distinction is irrelevant. He is legitimate in terms of succession and as he reveals, he is also personally suitable for kingship. He has been designated king by his father at the beginning of the play and having insisted on his depravity earlier in the scene, he now presents himself an almost saintly figure:

> I am yet
> Unknown to woman, never was forsworn,
> Scarcely have coveted what was mine own,
> At no time broke my faith, would not betray
> The devil to his fellow, and delight
> No less in truth than life.

> (4.3.125–30)

A coherent reading of this episode in terms of contemporary politics is almost impossible. The scene draws on myths and fantasies about kingship as well as serious political analysis of the extent of royal authority. It also raises questions about a king's own credibility since there is no dramatic time given either to corroborate or to deny Malcolm's assertions about himself. The scene seems to come from a different kind of play in which politics is more satirically and explicitly addressed.[6] Macduff, on the other hand, is given the opportunity to display both his political credentials in his response to Malcolm's revelations and his ethical and emotional power in his reaction to the news of his family's murder.

In that sequence, the play once again structures the dramatic action so as to locate political and military action alongside considerations of men's emotional and psychic relations. When Ross reluctantly concedes that Macduff's wife and children are dead, Macduff falls silent and his actions are described by Malcolm:

> What, man. Ne'er pull your hat upon your brows:
> Give sorrow words; the grief that does not speak
> Whispers the o'er-fraught heart, and bids it break.

> (4.3.209–11)

47

Macduff's silent reaction is one of the most powerful moments in Shakespeare's writing for it shows him resisting the temptation to give Macduff an eloquent, rhetorical expression for his sorrow. Rather he makes Macduff communicate by broken half lines with the single eloquent metaphor of the 'hell-kite' who had taken 'all my pretty chickens and their dam/At one fell swoop'(4.3.220). Macduff's reaction to his family's fate demonstrates Shakespeare's awareness of the dramatic power of silence, but the simple theatrical effect is also extended into a discussion of ideals of manhood as Malcolm urges Macduff to 'let grief convert to anger'. Macduff replies

> O I could play the woman with mine eyes,
> And braggart with my tongue.

> (4.3.232–3)

Eloquent language is associated with feminine weakness and duplicity. Earlier in the scene Macduff had made the gendered contrast between words and action explicit. Malcolm had urged 'Let us seek out some desolate shade, and there/Weep our sad bosoms empty'. Macduff responds that he would 'rather/ Hold fast the mortal sword and like good men/ Bestride our downfall birthdom [downfallen native land]' (4.3.1–4). Macduff's manhood is constructed in terms of a preference for action over words. As he says in his final battle with Macbeth, 'I have no words;/My voice is in my sword' (5.8.5–6).

This contrast between feminine garrulity and powerful male reticence echoes similar debates about manhood that had taken place between Macbeth and his lady over both the murder of Duncan and the ghost of Banquo. It provides the narrative and emotional impetus into the action of the play's finale and it is able to do so because it knits the questions of politics and kingship into the ethical debate over manliness and the nature of effective action.

The play as a whole dramatizes a dialectical relationship between these debates and their resolution in the action. This relationship suggests that the play's action, on balance, moves with the general direction of political evolution towards a definition of political authority residing in an inherited office, independent of but responsible to a people which extends beyond the nobility. The legitimacy of that political authority, nevertheless, can never be taken for granted and needs to be sustained by earlier relationships between kin, within families and in shifting definitions of manly action. The conflict in the play and the uncertainties of its resolution are, in part, a measure of that instability. The shifting dramatic relationship between politics, ethics and the emotions ensures the play's theatrical potential and emotional power in quite different political and historical worlds.

4

The Work in History

I have been suggesting that the 1623 text of *Macbeth*, read as a 'work', presents a story that is driven by suspense, that takes place in a social world extending beyond what is shown on stage and that creates characters whose contemplation of actions and their consequences raises complex ethical and psychic considerations. The text's figurative language, moreover, reinforces that narrative with patterns of recurring images that resonate with the physical images from the text's implied stage pictures. This match between the forward movement of the action and the local effects of scenes and poetry creates an aesthetically satisfying coherence that combines an exciting story with a sense of dealing with important ideas.

Such an account of the work, of course, depends upon the protocols of formalist literary criticism that were developed in the mid-twentieth century precisely to insist upon the integrity of works of literature. Practitioners of this critical method, the so-called New Critics, sought to show that the artistic effects of literary works were generated by their internal structure and could be understood and appreciated entirely in their own terms. Works of literature could thus take their place alongside works of plastic art and could share an aesthetic of form where symmetry and coherence were the most valued aspects of artistic effect.[1]

One important impulse behind New Criticism was a desire to rescue works of literature from the hands of pedants and philologists who sought to tie the meaning of literary works to arcane and specialized knowledge. In doing so they also rescued the literary work from its particular history. Like the artefacts in a museum, the work could be smoothed and polished by a critical process that emphasized its poetic coherence, relegating its connections to history to the footnotes.

As we have seen, the historical original of *Macbeth* was itself the product of a publishing process that created a literary version of the work, connected to but in no sense constrained by its prior existence as a play. No other text of the play exists, so the work of the 1623 Folio seems to provide a firm basis for the formalist reading that it both invites and rewards. In those circumstances, it might seem perverse to analyse too closely the work's relationship to history but for the fact that the formalist reading itself depends on a selected reference to history – a sense that the play inhabits a world from the past. Once we acknowledge that situation in history, the whole process unravels. An understanding of history does not negate the formalist reading but it does call into question its selective reading of history.

Behind the Folio text of the work, there was a play. In 1611, Simon Forman, the famous astrologer and magician, recorded a visit to *Macbeth* at the Globe Theatre, in 'The Bocke of Plaies and Notes therof per Common Pollicie'.[2] His account tells the story, much as it appears in the First Folio, from the opening prophecies to the king's murder, the murder of Banquo and his ghost's appearance at the feast, the murder of Macduff's wife and children and the final confrontation in which Macbeth is overthrown by the English forces.

Forman observed the relationship between motivation and action. Macbeth and Lady Macbeth were apparently 'moch amazed & Affronted' by their inability to wash Duncan's blood from their hands; and Macbeth's second murder was 'for feare of Banko, his old companion, that he should beget kinges but be no kinge him selfe'. Forman also notes particular theatrical moments, drawing attention to the bloody daggers and the sleepwalking scene and giving detailed attention to the appearance of Banquo's ghost. He notes the simple dramatic irony that the ghost appears at the very moment when Macbeth 'began to speak of Banquo and to wish that he were there' but he also notes the physical stage business with which the ghost's appearance was managed on the stage:

> As he thus did, standing up to drincke a Carouse to him, the ghoste
> of Banco came and sat down in his cheier behind him. And he

turning About to sit down Again sawe the goste of banco, which
fronted him so, that he fell into a great passion of fear and fury,
vtterynge many wordes about his murder by which, when they hard
that Banco was Murdred they Suspected Mackbet.[3]

Forman's attention to narrative and motivation is not surprising:
he used similar models of explanation throughout his scientific
diary, his notes on his patients and his autobiography. As far as
Forman's notes were concerned, this play was not a story of
witches and kings but a play in which prophecy was fulfilled. It
was more of a revenge play that followed a logic of tit for tat: 'In
the meantyme whylle Macdovee was in England, Mackbet
slewe Mackdoves wife & children, and after in the battelle
Mackdove slewe Mackbet'. The figures who prophecy the future
to Macbeth and Banquo are not witches but '3 women feiries or
Nimphes' and he makes no mention of the final witch scene,
with its apparitions, prophecies and the parade of kings.

Forman's account of the play in the theatre need not
undermine the significance of the work that appeared in the
Folio text. The practice of adding material for the printed
version of a play, turning a play into a 'work' was highlighted by
many of Shakespeare's contemporaries. Moreover the analysis
of Shakespeare's plays that exist in multiple texts shows the
writer adding progressively more poetry to the theatrical
outline, sometimes more than could have been played in the
'two hours traffic' of theatre performance.[4] Forman's account of
the play, nevertheless, does raise questions about the terms in
which the work has been and can be connected to its history.

History is most often invoked when the work seems to be at
odds with the expectations of later readers. Dr Johnson, who
created a new *Complete Works of Shakespeare* in 1755, appended a
long and learned note to the opening stage direction of *Macbeth*,
'Enter three witches'. In it, he summarized what was then
known about the history of witchcraft and dealt in particular
with King James's interest in witchcraft and his involvement in
the trials of the witches interrogated at Berwick in 1590–1. Dr
Johnson used this information about the history of witchcraft to
protect Shakespeare from the charge of foolish superstition, an
accusation that might well have come from Johnson himself. He
feared that his eighteenth century contemporaries might regard
a play about witches as the mark of a writer who was fit only to

'be banished from the Theatre to the nursery, and condemned to write fairy tales instead of tragedies.'[5] Johnson suggested instead that Shakespeare was working within a 'system that was then universally admitted to his advantage, and was far from overburthening the credulity of his audience'.

Johnson's historicizing impulse was an understandable reaction to the critical assumptions of his time. Like all critics since, he wished to protect the play from inappropriate and unhistorical judgements about its value. The connection he makes between belief in witchcraft and King James's interests allowed him to suggest that if the monarch could credit witchcraft, its cultural significance could be assured. By noting the connection between James's own writing on witchcraft and the cases of the Berwick witches, interrogated in James's Scottish court and popularized in a pamphlet called *Newes from Scotland* in 1597, Johnson developed both the scholarship and a method for reading the play which has lasted until the present day. The play, as a consequence, was lifted out of the entertainment and publishing industries of its time and turned into a representative work of history. It required its reader to suspend his own taste and to make the effort to understand the play's value in historical terms.

Those historical terms, of course, remained closely tied to the work itself in a self reinforcing cycle that made the literary work a way into history and history a source of a more refined appreciation of the work. The work was connected to the royal court, by virtue of Shakespeare's membership of the King's Men playing company as well as James's alleged interest in demonology. That connection was thought to assure the play's connection to contemporary politics and therefore its significance in the cultural life of the nation. Historical evidence, such as Forman's account, that suggested that at least one spectator saw no connection between the play and the concern with witches and kings, was not available to Dr Johnson and was largely ignored in the critical tradition that he established.

Dr Johnson's suggestions that difficulties in the play could be elucidated by reference to history, has provided a useful paradigm from which to explain the many difficult passages that remain in the Folio text. The need for this historical paradigm seems especially pressing in those rare moments when the immediate meaning of the play's text eludes our grasp entirely. One such moment is the speech by the Porter who enters the stage in response to the knocking that ends the scene between Macbeth and his lady after the murder of Duncan.

The knocking at the gate at the end of Macbeth and his lady's frantic reflections on the deed of murder startles both the conspirators and the audience. It provides another opportunity to contrast Lady Macbeth's calm pragmatism – 'A little water clears us of this deed... Get on your night-gown' (2.2.70–3) – with Macbeth's guilt stricken symbolic reading of the event: 'Wake Duncan with thy knocking: I would thou couldst' (2.2.77). The Porter is both practical and comically portentous, presenting himself as playing the role of 'porter of hell gate', listing the people who might be sent there.

The Porter's monologue has been felt to require extensive editorial commentary to explain obscure references and lost jokes. It has also come to play a crucial role in the arguments about dating the play and elaborating its connection to the politics of the time. The jokes can, of course, be explained by editorial glossing that need not go beyond the particular moment in the text. For example, the Porter refers to 'an equivocator', one whose language deals in deliberate ambiguity that cannot be pinned down to incriminate the speaker; an 'English tailor... stealing out of a French hose' (2.3.12–13) would have been skimping on material and his 'goose' was his iron. 'Beelzebub' was one of the devils who accompanied Satan when he fell from heaven and the 'everlasting bonfire' is a jokey reference to hell itself. The Porter's lines about 'a farmer that hanged himself on th'expectation of plenty' (2.3.3–4) refers to the practice of 'engrossing' grain, keeping it back from the market until the price rises during a period of shortage. The farmer hangs himself because he expects that 'plenty' – a good harvest – will make grain prices fall.

When each word is understood, the theatrical point of the passage is clear. The Porter is speaking directly to the audience, describing the parade of malefactors on their way to hell. It has to be said that the speech is not very funny and when it is included in performance, like most written clowning speeches, it requires some actorly ingenuity to make it effective on the stage. As a result it seems to undermine the sense of coherent work 'for all time' by presenting a set of obscure in-jokes that seems too tightly tied to the contemporary world outside the play. As a result, the speech and the character were dropped completely from some later versions of the play and some commentators have concluded that the speech could not have been written by Shakespeare and was merely a distraction interpolated by the actors. Others have drawn attention to the references to hell and to the motif of equivocation in both the witches' speeches and in Macbeth's response to them, claiming that it plays an integral part in creating the play's moral and political world. For a fifteen-line prose speech, it has attracted a disproportionate amount of commentary.

The extensive commentary on the Porter's speech, like discussions of the witches, demonstrates the uneasy critical relationship between the work and its history. A feature of the work's artistic pattern is felt to require explanation because it does not fit later taste. That explanation then becomes the basis for an overdetermined view of the play as a whole. On the whole, modern critics and editors take the view that the Porter's speech is a significant part of the play that engages in dynamic commentary on the political and ethical world of early modern England. That critical commonplace, however, needs to be unravelled.

Whether we assume that the Porter's monologue was written by Shakespeare or interpolated by the actors or another playwright, the topical references offered a brief set piece, a short introductory solo for a clown that might have flattered some of the London audience's knowledge of current affairs.[6] The fact that Simon Forman makes no reference to such an episode, though not conclusive, might also suggest that the speech could be removed when the references lost their topicality. Topicality, however, offers the alluring temptation of fixing the play in history, dating it precisely and speculating about the impact of the whole play on contemporary audiences.

For example, the Porter's reference to the engrossing farmer has been read as a reference to the particularly low price of wheat in 1605–7. That date coincides neatly with the trials of the Gunpowder plotters early in 1606 and in particular with the trial of Henry Garnet on March 28 in that year. The 'equivocator...

who committed treason enough for God's sake', could refer to Henry Garnet, who used equivocation (the practice of blurring the distinction between different kinds of truth) as part of his defence when he was tried for treason as one of the conspirators in the Gunpowder plot to assassinate King James. The loop into historical significance seems secure. However, the kind of historical thinking behind this connection is dangerously loose. It assumes that the co-existence of two events implies their connection, a procedure warned against by Shakespeare himself. When Glendower in *1 Henry IV* claims that the 'frame and huge foundation of the earth/Shak'd like a coward' when he was born, Hotspur replies

> Why, so it would have done
> At the same season if your mother's cat
> Had but kittened

(1HIV, 3.1.15–17)

A more historically scrupulous study suggests rather different results. In his ground breaking analysis of 'Shakespeare without King James',[7] J. Leeds Barroll has undertaken a detailed analysis of the sequence of dates in the progress of the Gunpowder plotters' trial, identifying the opportunities for playing when the theatres would not have been closed, either by plague restrictions or the observation of Lent. He observes that '*Macbeth* could have played at a public theatre between April 21 and June or July'.[8] That conclusion could date the Porter's set piece if its immediate topicality were to be insisted upon, but it need not extend into the dating of the whole of the rest of the play.

Tracking the precise relationships between topical events and their appearance in a play published some eighteen years later is an altogether more difficult task. As Leeds Barroll shows, the desire to date the whole play in relation to the politics of the Gunpowder plot, depends on assumptions about the play having a special relationship to King James. There *was* a date in August when the play could have been presented before King James, during the visit of the King of Denmark, when three plays were ordered from the King's Men. However, even if *Macbeth* had been one of the plays shown on this occasion, there is no proof that the play was written with this event in mind. As Barroll concludes

The nature of royal ceremonial movements... and the ever-present possibility of cancellations would make it difficult for Shakespeare to pick a particular play for a particular occasion. One can only claim *Macbeth* for the evening of the Gowry anniversary through observing that by an interesting coincidence Shakespeare happened to have a play ready that seemed a perfect fit.[9]

Dating the play in a direct relationship to political questions also ignores some uncomfortable counter-evidence. In 1600, six years before the trials of the Gunpowder plotters, William Kemp, the clown from Shakespeare's company, referred to meeting a 'penny poet' whose 'first making was the stolen story of Macdoel, or Macdobeth, or Macsomewhat'. This reference corroborates a suggestion, added to the record of the Court of the Stationers Company of fining a printer for printing a ballad without permission, that a 'ballad of Macdobeth' existed as early as 1596. Ballad versions of plays tended to be published after the plays had been performed, a way of capitalizing on their popularity, so it may suggest that the play of *Macbeth*, by Shakespeare or another writer, existed long before the accession of James or the events of the Gunpowder plot.[10] This hint of an earlier version, however, is seldom taken seriously in dating the play. This is partly because the style of the play, as we shall see, is very different from that of Shakespeare's earlier work.

The rejection of an earlier dating is, of course, critically connected to a desire to associate Shakespeare's plays with the court politics of King James VI and I. That connection is usually asserted on the basis of the company's change of name, from the Lord Chamberlain's Men to the King's Men soon after James's accession to the throne. Barroll assesses the evidence and suggests that there is little to suggest that re-naming Shakespeare's company as the King's Men was any more than a minor favour granted to their supporters at court and none to show that James himself took any personal interest in playing.[11] Moreover, theatrical performances played only a minor part in court life, as court entertainment was restricted to the periods of festivity surrounding the court season from November to Lent and the choice of plays for those occasions was a matter for the Master of the Revels. *Macbeth* in particular is not recorded as a play performed at court and there is no direct evidence that the play had any purchase in the court's political affairs.

We must seek elsewhere for an understanding of the contemporary sources of Shakespeare's references to topical events. 'The farmer that hang'd himself on the expectation of plenty' does refer to the life-world of the uncertainty of early modern agriculture and its frequent grain shortages. The frequent fluctuation in grain prices, however, makes such a supposed event inconsequential for dating the play. Moreover an engrossing farmer had also been seen in a black comic sequence in Ben Jonson's *Everyman Out of his Humour* (3.2.) where he comes on stage *'with a halter about his neck'* because of the drop in the price of grain. Shakespeare himself performed in that play in 1598 and the King's Men had revived it at court in 1604.[12] The engrossing farmer was a familiar enough social type to be included in the Porter's speech as a comic gesture in a list of those going to hell without there being a particular topical reference. The theatrical reference is likely to be as memorable as any real-life example.

The equivocator, too, though associated with Catholic practice had a wider social and theological remit than a direct reference to Henry Garnet himself. Recent historical writing on the Gunpowder plot reveals the huge gap that exists between the experience of historical events and their potential for incorporation into a play. The Gunpowder plot was a highly complex political and historical event that remains controversial to this day. The plotters seem to have been members of a radical group who harboured desperate frustration at the lack of progress in James's toleration of Catholics. In this, their political views were different from the majority of loyalist Catholics who accepted the separation of spiritual and temporal power and remained faithful to the English crown.[13] The abortive Gunpowder plot was a disappointment to many Catholics, not because it failed to assassinate James and Members of Parliament, but because it provided a focus for anti-Catholic sentiments and justified further anti-Catholic penal laws.[14]

The connection between equivocation and the discussion of religion and politics, had existed long before the events of the Gunpowder plot. It can be identified in the play because of the way that the motif of equivocation is found in its thematic and verbal structures. The echoing antithesis of 'fair' and 'foul' in the witches' opening incantation is unnervingly picked up in

Macbeth's first lines of the play; we find, as the witches suggest, that the battle has been both 'lost and won' and their prophecy to Banquo, that sets 'lesser' against 'greater', 'not so happy' against 'happier' offers a set of equivocal alternatives which are nonetheless fulfilled as the play unfolds. In his subsequent soliloquy, too, Macbeth takes on the witches' equivocating style of speech, musing that 'This supernatural soliciting /Cannot be ill; cannot be good', and concluding 'And nothing is, but what is not' (1.3.129–30; 140–1).

Equivocation, along with other forms of illusionism and prestidigitation was associated in protestant polemic with Catholic theology and religious practice. Unsympathetic Protestants regarded the Catholic doctrine of the 'true presence', in which the communion bread and wine actually embodied the body and blood of Christ, as a kind of sleight of hand, associated with magic tricks and juggling. This gives an added resonance to Macbeth's angry final rejection of the witches' practice as the action of 'juggling fiends'.

The witches' juggling and 'double sense' can be read as a type of heretical equivocation. It asserts a truth in words which cannot be fulfilled in deed. It deals in half-truths and paradox much as Catholics were thought to be able to promise allegiance to the temporal powers of the realm while at the same time denying its spiritual authority. As Alison Shell has shown, for intellectual Catholics, equivocation involved a genuine intellectual questioning of the relationship between abstract ideals of loyalty to the monarch and commitment to the policies of a particular king:

> It does most of them a disservice to equate Catholicism with subversion... it was their aim to re-integrate tributes to Caesar with those to God, and most would have hoped that this could be accomplished by the conversion of the reigning monarch.[15]

Stuart Clark, the historian of witchcraft and belief, has described how the controversy over equivocation was extended to include early-modern debates on the nature of sight and seeing. He shows how Banquo's ghost and the vision of the dagger are both connected to questions of the veracity of things seen and the ethical concern with their true interpretation.

At this time intellectuals were rethinking the fundamentals of vision and debating, in particular, the very extent to which sight was a constructed medium – constructed, that is, in terms of perceptual systems... that made the eye not the innocent reporter of the world but its creator and interpreter.[16]

Clark discusses a telling connection between Macbeth and Pierre Le Loyer's treatise on vision, *Quatre Livres des Spectres* published in 1586 and, in an enlarged edition, in 1608. The first section was published in English as 'A treatise of spectres and straunge sights' and includes examples of tyrants who, like Macbeth, were visited at supper by the ghosts of those they had murdered. Le Loyer actually includes the story of Macbeth in Book 2 of his treatise, though since this was never published in English it is unlikely to be a direct source for Shakespeare's play. As Clark explains, the existence of the Macbeth story in this collection suggests that there was a connection between Macbeth's experience of ghosts and apparitions and the wider debate about the ethical reliability of sight. This question of ethical reliability was further connected with politics through the close affiliation between truth and the vision of the godly magistrate. Macbeth's faulty interpretation of visions, like his false and wilful belief in the witches' prophecies was another of the characteristic actions which denied him the authority of a true king.

The complexity of Clark's argument, his careful elaboration of a network of connections between disparate elements of written intellectual culture and theological analysis, makes it a model for ways of reading a Shakespeare play in terms of contemporary cultural politics. It demonstrates the inadequacy of a monologic reading which merely points to possible verbal connections or topical analogies between the play and contemporary events. The play cannot be 'about' the Gunpowder plot or the Stuart succession; nor can information about the Gunpowder plot or the Stuart succession stand in for the experience of the play. Rather, the play and its cultural moment co-exist in time and share wide-ranging beliefs, assumptions and preoccupations. These beliefs may inform but cannot substitute for the language and narrative and structure of feeling of the play.

The relationship of contemporary ideas to the abstracted version of the play's themes remains at the heart of the critical process, nevertheless. The complexity and uncertainty that surrounds it is created by the fact that both plays and the historical world in which they came to life were in a state of movement, subject to controversy and hotly contested. It is impossible to resolve a critical controversy by invoking contemporary beliefs, since contemporary beliefs were debated and subject to change. Although it is clear that James VI and I, King of England and Scotland, did not take much personal interest in *Macbeth*, it is undoubtedly the case that the play echoes controversies about kingship that were being addressed in contemporary historical writing. Indeed, by writing a play set in the deep past of the Scottish nation, Shakespeare was making an intervention in historical controversy.

As we have seen, the shape of his story and its articulation by his characters emphasized its ethical and emotional dimension rather than offering a systematic political analysis. But as well as the story of Macbeth the tyrant, the play also hints at a wider narrative of modernization: a move from the almost magical relations of blood and kin to the more structured dispersal of power proposed by Malcolm when he declares, at the end of the play, that the thanes shall become earls.

Historians of kingship have described four distinct, but overlapping, phases in the development of models of monarchy from mediaeval to early modern times:

> The most primitive form may be designated as pre-feudal: politics based on blood and kinship relationships. Secondly, the feudal form: relationships still based on personal obligation but no longer necessarily confined to familial ties... Thirdly, the position of the king is enhanced... kings attempted to elevate themselves from a feudal role of *primus inter pares* among the elite and to reduce their contractual obligations... Fourthly there was the growth of institutional politics, fed by several sources. The elevation of the king highlighted the probable gap between the fallibility of the actual king and the infallibility of his office... Kingship became institutionalised, that is, the king could act impersonally, he could not die and he could do no wrong.[17]

The ending of *Macbeth* seems to situate Malcolm's political resolution in the change between the first and second phases of this development: relationships still based on personal obligation but no longer necessarily confined to familial ties. Political ideas in the Jacobean period, on the other hand, were debating the transition between phases three and four: between institutional politics and absolutism.

These debates over the nature of kingship had a particular political purchase in the context of a newly succeeded king whose claim to the throne had been a matter for debate and political concern in the reign of an unmarried queen who left no heir. In 1595, the Catholic controversialist, Robert Parsons, had published 'A Conference about the next succession to the Crown of England'. In it he had argued that though James's right to the throne 'by nearness of succession' was not in dispute, there were nevertheless 'reasons enough to frustrate and overthrow this claim and pretension'.[18] Parsons's argument showed that other models of kingship existed and that rights of succession depended on varied combinations of subjects' rights and legal precedent, all of which depended ultimately on the truth that 'God disposeth of kingdoms and worketh his will in Princes affairs as he pleaseth, and this by extraordinary means'. Parsons's arguments were countered by other writers who supported James's claim to the throne. Sir John Hayward, for example, insisted that 'in most nations of the world, the people have lost all power of election, and succession is firmly settled in one descent'. So strong was his belief in descent that he insisted that succession should follow without reference to the personal attributes of the actual heir:

> It is somewhat inconvenient (I grant) to be governed by a Prince either impotent or evil, but it is a greater inconvenience, by making a breach into this high point of state, to open the way to all manner of ambitions, perjuries, cruelties and spoils...But so soon as the king departeth out of life, the royalty is presently transferred to the next succecssor, according to the laws and customs of the realm.[19]

It is easy to see through the logic of Hayward's case which attributes ambitions, perjuries, cruelties and spoils to a king elected by the people and not to one succeeding to the throne. Nevertheless his reference to 'the laws and customs of the realm' shows that his argument, like Parsons's, worked within a broad framework which set legal precedent against common law and subsumed both under the will of God. These were the classic defences of the contemporary model of kingship but by intersecting them with ideals of kingly authority based on kinship and communal values sealed by feasting and gifts, the play turns political questions into ethical and emotional ones.

These issues are never explicitly debated in the play. However they do resonate with the political problems of the reign of James VI and I. James's donations of money and annuities to his Scottish followers, which caused so much concern and mockery among his English subjects, can be seen as an attempt to extend the structures of allegiance, which had supported him in Scotland, into his foreign kingdom. James needed to maintain the support of his nobles since the Union of the Crowns was a purely dynastic extension of James's personal rule; it united neither church nor state and the legal and ecclesiastical systems remained distinct.[20] In building political support in England, James followed both the traditional methods of buying the nobles' allegiance and at the same time began to develop the institutional relationships of a modern state.

The process of establishing James's legitimacy and authority was further compromised by endemic English hostility to the Scots. This hostility involved not only distrust of James as king but also a sense of the primitive character of Scottish kingship. A good deal of the resentment against a Scottish king arose from the fact that for many English people Scotland was regarded as backward and yet infuriatingly resistant to English imperialism.[21] In a notorious speech in Parliament, Sir Christopher Piggot alleged that the Scots 'have not suffered above two kings to die in their beds, these two hundred years'.[22] In reminding Parliament that murder had been a common mode of succession in Scotland, Piggot was calling into question not only the Scots' ethical authority but also the modernity of their ideas of kingship. His assertion was historically correct, but it also drew on long-standing historical debates conditioned by the need to articulate the relative rights and strengths of Scots and English kingship in pursuit of the ancient conflict between the two nations.

This political conflict bears on *Macbeth* in that early versions of the story, that informed the narratives Shakespeare consulted, had been used to emphasize 'the continuity of Scottish kingship to counter English claims of historical overlordship'[23] and began the isolation of Macbeth as an exceptional murderous tyrant. Shakespeare may or may not have been directly engaged by this controversy but its existence suggests a political context for the play that informed some of the sources that he consulted for his account of the play.

Shakespeare found the story of Macbeth in the *History of Scotland* which was part of the great compilation of 'the chronicles of England, Scotland and Ireland' including 'The description and chronicles of Scotland, from the first originall of the Scottes nation, till the year 1571'. Holinshed's chronicle was a large and old-fashioned compendium of stories quite different from the new historiography that fuelled the political debates of the time. Nevertheless, its organization according to the nations that made up the British archipelago and its concern for national difference gave it a coherence and a political perspective that went beyond purely sequential narrative.

In the chronicle of Scotland, for example, Shakespeare could have found not only the tale of Macbeth and Banquo meeting with the witches but a discussion of the power of witches to be 'the cause of much trouble in the realme of Scotland' and of repeated unsuccessful efforts to control them. The Scotland described in Holinshed was one that was emerging with some conflict out of the realm of magic and into a world of recognizable political power. In Holinshed, the trio who greet Macbeth are not village witches from the seventeenth century but 'three women in strange and wild apparel, resembling creatures of elder world'. The chronicle-writer later speculates uncertainly about their exact nature and the quality of their prophecy:

> But afterwards the common opinion was, that these women were either the weird sisters, that is (as ye would say) the goddesses of destinie, or else some nymphs or feiries, indued with the knowledge of prophesie by their necromanticall science.[24]

A similar uncertainty echoes around the chronicler's discussion of the inheritance practices of the time that he describes. When Holinshed writes of Macbeth's disappointment that Duncan has named the prince of Cumberland as his successor, he is aware that Duncan's act is in breach of 'the old lawes of the realm (where) the ordinance was, that if he that should succeed were not of able age to take the charge upon himselfe, he that was next of blood unto him should be admitted'.[25]

The chronicler presents a narrative that is driven partly by the strange practice of the Scottish people, partly by Macbeth's sense of injury at being deprived of the crown and partly by 'the words of the three weird sisters'. Macbeth's wife, too, is given her share in the motivation, 'as she that was verie ambitious, burning in unquenchable desire to beare the name of a queene'.[26]

Shakespeare's version of the story echoes some of the ambiguities in Holinshed but it also keeps the narrative line clear by simply omitting Holinshed's account of the ten year gap between the murder of Duncan and Macbeth's defeat by the English forces. During this period, Holinshed notes, Macbeth

> used great liberalitie towards the nobles of the realm, thereby to win their favour, and when he saw that no man went about to trouble him, he set his whole intention to mainteine justice, and to punish all enormities and abuses, which had chanced through the feeble and slouthfull administration of Duncane.[27]

Holinshed's emphasis on Macbeth's good governance, turns the dark age warrior into a modern, institutional king, responsible for the well-being of all the people and attending to the proper conduct of the church, all of which he assures by legal and constitutional means.[28] However Holinshed's Macbeth is also a king in the machiavellian mode. His good legal and constitutional work is presented as a way of ensuring his strategic position, 'a counterfet zeale of equitie shewed by him, partlie against his natural inclination to purchase thereby the favour of the people.'[29] Once he had consolidated his position, his fear of revenge made him behave in a tyrannical fashion, first putting the nobles to death in order to enrich his coffers 'by their goods which were forfeited to his use', and then building his castle at Dunsinane by forced labour and subventions from his nobles. His conflict with Macduff arose, according to Holinshed, because of Macduff's refusal to attend to the building of Dunsinane in person.

Holinshed's account of Macbeth's history drew on earlier histories and it reveals the way that his definitions of good and bad kingship depended on a curious mixture of personal allegiance, legal instruments and respect for the nobles' autonomy. The attention to 'wholesome laws and statutes' suggests a model of institutional monarchy but the idea of Macbeth as 'defense and buckler' of innocent people, equally draws on much older ideas of the king as protector. The insistence on churchmen attending divine service echoes a post-reformation sense that good ecclesiastical governance depended on the monarch, while the dispute over forced labour and the appropriation of nobles' goods is an example of the feudal conflict over the respective rights of nobles and kings.

The writing of history for Holinshed as much as Shakespeare was always a dialogue between knowledge of the past and the concerns of the present. One did not overwhelm the other and, in Shakespeare's creative construction of a new kind of historical work, it is possible to see the writer sharing his contemporaries' interests in narratives from the past, reworking and refining the language and poetry with which he dramatizes his characters' dilemmas and adapting the typically renaissance mix of learning and hearsay, proverbs and myths into the speeches and situations that make up the play.

The same complex interconnection existed between the multiple views of witchcraft identified in Holinshed, the experience of witchcraft in the world that Shakespeare and his audience knew, and the ways that it was written about by contemporaries. In this arena as much as in the arena of politics, the insistence on a direct relationship between the play and James VI and I's interests has obscured the dynamic dialogue among these historical forces, not least in relation to King James's own engagement with witchcraft debates.

Christina Larner has pointed out there were three distinct phases of James's relationship with witch prosecutions:

> James was relatively uninterested in demonology until 1590, intensely interested from the sorcery trials of 1590 until the publication of his *Demonologie* in 1597, and slightly embarrassed and anxious to make the least of his former enthusiasm thereafter.[30]

By the time *Macbeth* was being written, in other words, James was distancing himself from his earlier enthusiasm for witch-craft prosecutions which had become dangerously polarized by the religious politics of the new reign. Witchcraft as a matter of state policy and judicial practice was less a matter of settled belief and more a fluid process of interaction between elite theology and village behaviour which occasionally came to the attention of the authorities. It was, in Larner's useful formulation, an epiphenomenon of religious and intellectual controversy that intersected at particular moments with customary practice and became the focus of the judicial and religious authorities' efforts to establish their control over the population. James's interest as represented in the *Demonologie* was undoubtedly an important element in the development of Scottish writing on witchcraft. However, Larner has pointed out that it was a derivative work, heavily dependent on Reginald Scot's *Discovery of Witchcraft*, the principal sceptical critique of contemporary witchcraft written in English. James had set out to refute Reginald Scot but at a mere 80 pages in length, his work can hardly be seen as a significant contribution to an intellectual debate that had preoccupied some of the major thinkers in Europe.

James's connection to witch belief was highlighted by the notorious case of the witches of Berwick in 1590 in which he took a personal interest, including commanding them to appear at the royal court. His interest may have been aroused because the accusations against them included an alleged attempt on his own life. Local practice had become treason. Even more significant was the fact that James had returned from a visit to the Danish court. As well as collecting his bride there, he had spent time engaged in learned discussion with Danish theologians, experts in the continental demonology which had provided the intellectual rationale for the much more deadly witch trials in Europe.

The initial charges that witches had caused the gales which almost drowned the king and queen on their return from Denmark were initially made on the Danish side of the North Sea, but similar accusations were levelled at their Scottish counterparts, probably initiated by James himself. Unravelling the resulting murderous mix of local prejudice, clashing personalities, theological disputes and national politics is a daunting task for historical anthropologists: what it cannot do is to provide a simple line from a Scottish witch trial to the reception of an English play written over a decade later.

That line is complicated by Shakespeare's own possible awareness of the Scottish witch material and his use of it to

67

create some of the play's effects. His source for that awareness came from a pamphlet published in 1597 calling itself *Newes from Scotland*. It was only tangentially connected to the 1590–1 trials of the witches of Berwick: its language and references to legal processes show that it must have been produced in England rather than Scotland, one of a series of news stories of witch trials published at the turn of the century. Nonetheless, it provided Shakespeare with some of the images and ideas that he included in the play and some that he did not. Setting the pamphlet against the play can reveal some of the raw material from which the play was created.

The pamphlet's woodcut frontispiece includes the image of women round a cauldron that may have suggested the cauldron scene of 4.1. and its picture of a ship may have suggested the shipwreck invoked in the witches' speeches in 1.3. The pamphlet also alleges that Agnes Thompson, one of the witches accused by King James, gathered the venom from a toad to poison the king. It may have suggested the image of the 'toad that under cold stone/days and nights hath thirty one/sweltered venom sleeping got' (4.1.6–9) that is thrown into the witches pot in 4.1. This direct verbal parallel shows that Shakespeare probably knew the pamphlet, but as the writer of a play he seems to have been more concerned to write a different kind of witch narrative than the pamphlet was able to offer him.

The pamphlet tells the story of the witches of Berwick who were accused of conspiring with a schoolmaster, Dr Fian, to conjure up the devil, and were examined by King James himself. The story follows the familiar form of many contemporary witch pamphlets that structured stories of witches around suspicious behaviour and inexplicable disasters followed by discovery, interrogation and condemnation of the witches. Shakespeare's play does not follow that narrative form: there is no doubt that his witches are witches and their opening prophecy, that Macbeth will be Thane of Cawdor, is immediately corroborated by events so no narrative time needs to be given to uncovering them as the source of mysterious events. As we have seen, the witches' prophecies are critical to the play's structure, but as Forman's account shows, their structural role was achieved, in the version he saw, by their role as prophets.

Forman's account of the play raises the intriguing possibility that the more extended role for the witches, particularly in the cauldron and apparitions scene may have been added when the play was prepared for print. It may, in other words, have been part of the process of turning the play into a work.[31] Forman's witches simply salute Macbeth as Thane of Cawdor and tell him that 'thou shalt be a king but shall beget no kings' and tell Banquo that 'thou shalt beget kings, yet be no king'. In the version of the play that was printed in the Folio, on the other hand, the witches' speeches create the sense that more is at stake in this play than a dynastic conflict in dark-age Scotland. The gap between Forman's memory of a performance and the final version of the play provides an intriguing possibility of a writer changing his mind, drawing on new material, taken from tales of village witchcraft and from learned witchlore.

The witches' speeches in the Folio have an allusive, open-ended character that beckons towards a wider culture but never quite reveals the way in. Their opening dialogue invokes but does not identify a world beyond the play from which they come. They know about the battle, lost and won; they plan to meet someone called Macbeth but do not tell us why or whether they are meeting someone new. When they reappear in 1.3. they briefly give the reader more, and more mysterious, information. The reference to the witches 'killing swine' (1.3.2) is a commonplace of village witch accusations but their plan to victimize the sailor whose wife refused them the chestnuts gives a vivid particularity to the familiar idea that witches could persecute people and cause them to sicken inexplicably. The image of the witches attacking a sailor may have come from the frontispiece of *Newes from Scotland* that shows a wrecked ship – an obvious accusation against witches from Berwick, a coastal town whose harbour is still notoriously dangerous to enter. The speech with its regular rhythm and insistent rhyme combines the abstract idea that witches control the wind with the chanting incantation of

> I'll drain him dry as hay:
> Sleep shall neither night nor day
> Hang upon his penthouse lid:
> He shall live a man forbid:
> Weary sennights nine times nine,
> Shall he dwindle, peak, and pine:

Though his bark cannot be lost,
Yet it shall be tempest-tossed.

(1.3.17–24)

The incantation continues with the business of the pilot's thumb and the connection back to Macbeth's story is seamlessly effected within the rhyme scheme but with the added excitement of a drumbeat sound effect:

FIRST WITCH. Here I have a pilots thumb,
    Wrecked as homeward he did come.
                Drum within.
THIRD WITCH. A Drum, a Drum;
    Macbeth doth come.

(1.3.29–32)

The sense that the witches are mysterious and sinister is created by dramatic and poetic devices rather than being simply transported from contemporary belief. Similar poetic devices are used in Act 4. There, the witches are even more strange as their language moves away from killing swine and tormenting a sailor's wife to the dangerous world associated with a list of poisonous and alien creatures and the body parts of demonized peoples, the Jew, the Tartar, and the Turk. The notorious list of the cauldron's ingredients gains its particular poetic effect from the evocative detail as the rhyme and rhythm that emphasizes first the creatures that the parts come from (newt, frog; bat, dog) and then the part that will be taken (fork, sting; leg, wing). The first set of images is familiar but then the speech moves into a list of obscure and exotic objects:

Scale of dragon, tooth of wolf,
Witches' mummy, maw, and gulf
Of the ravined salt-sea shark:
Root of hemlock, digged i'th' dark:

(4.1.22–5)

In the latter part of the invocation, the list briefly extends beyond the formula of a body item and a possessive noun, into verbs that give some indication of an action that secured them. The hemlock is 'digged i'th' dark', suggesting once again the witches' off-stage life, and the evocation of the 'finger of birth-strangled babe/ditch-delivered by a drab' (4.1.30–1) offers a

70

telling glimpse of a grim social world in which infanticide might have been the desperate conclusion of unauthorized sexual relations. Extraordinary poetic skill goes into this famous episode to create its tantalizing evocation of a social world that is just out of sight. For generations of critics, it has appeared to beckon towards an irresistible route into the social history of early modern England, matching the play's imaginative power with a wider ethical or imaginative engagement with the lives of women in early modern England. The image of the birth-strangled babe can be connected to the 'bloody babe' that the witches show Macbeth. However, it also opens up the critical possibility of a further link between the witches, Lady Macbeth's invocation of the spirits that tend on mortal thoughts, the sexual dynamic of the confrontation between Macbeth and his lady, and the fate of the birth-strangled babe's unacknowledged mother.[32]

The witches' speeches offer vivid local detail but, unlike the witchcraft pamphlets, they have no developed narrative of their own. As a result, discussion of the witches in the play always leads away from its action into the realms of social history and the history of early-modern scientific and theological ideas. That arena of knowledge is fascinating in its own right but it cannot provide a stable base from which to understand the role of the witches in the play. It is impossible to close off the witches' mystery by invoking either generalized accounts of early-modern witch beliefs, or analogies with other witch cases.

Though the witches in *Macbeth* have undoubtedly played a part in generating historical interest in early English witchcraft, modern social historians emphasize that the belief and practice of witchcraft varies significantly across the period and is different from place to place. Increasingly social historians examine local conditions, such as the arrival of a new land-owner, a reforming minister or a commissioned witch-finder in creating the different crises that resulted in witch accusations and trials across the period. Historians of witchcraft have emphasized the way in which cases of witchcraft that caught the attention of local justices or metropolitan pamphlet writers were as much the construction of the observers of witch practices as they were objective accounts of actual events. Whether the actions of a particular witch were dismissed as superstition, tried as maleficium in a church court, or gloated over as a tall tale of village life by London readers, depended on who was telling the story and to whom it was told.

Analysis of a range of these cases has emphasized that witch belief was a complex of intellectual traditions which included significant resistance to superstition and the varied local beliefs that implicated the victims as much as the accused. Witchcraft was both an engine of elite control of popular belief and what Clive Holmes has called 'an outlet for personal feelings that would not otherwise achieve sanctioned expression – sexual fantasies, religious doubts, rage at parents, frustration with constrictions imposed by social and gender roles'.[33] In his magisterial account of witch-belief, Stuart Clark has emphasized that witchcraft in early modern England involved less a conflict between belief and scepticism than an understanding of the relative functions of belief and scepticism in emergent ideas about the relationship between human beings and nature. He locates the debates over witchcraft as part of a contest over the nature of evidence within theology and natural philosophy. By demonstrating the consistency between witch belief and other intellectual analyses, he removes the issue of witchcraft from the credulous superstitions of early-modern people into legitimate early-modern modes of thought.[34]

Stuart Clark's intellectual approach is helpful for understanding the relationship between witch sources and Shakespeare's play. He emphasizes that witch belief was a matter of intellectual interpretation as much as superstitious horror and it is this intellectual complexity that informs the handling of the witch material in Shakespeare's play. It is impossible to tell how far Shakespeare was actually aware of either the learned controversy or particular cases of witchcraft accusations. What is clear is that the open-endedness of the debate and the multitude of visual and narrative materials available provided a rich resource that made witchcraft a live and open question to be used by a writer who may have polished a play into a work.

Banquo, for example, wonders 'can the devil speak true' (1.3.105) and gravely warns Macbeth that 'to win us to their harm,/The instruments of darkness tell us truths' (1.3.122–3). These questions were central to the interpretation of witches that informed the contemporary pamphlet literature and they were echoed in the constant insistence on the part of pamphlet writers that their stories, unlike all the others, were true. The strand in witchcraft sources that contrasts low-life superstitition with theological belief, thus provides the central irony of the play but the details of those narratives, their concern with judicial processes or the movement from disbelief to condemnation, is left unused.

For the purposes of the play's narrative, the attention is less on the witches than on their prophecy. By allowing his witches to prophesy, Shakespeare was effectively combining two traditions. Low life female folk witches were seldom accorded the dignity of prophecy – that was the prerogative of men[35] or the quasi-supernatural classical figures such as the sybils who greeted King James on his entrance to St John's College, Oxford in 1604.[36] By crossing the learned tradition of classical prophecy and the vivid detail of village witchcraft practice, Shakespeare achieves the combination of narrative force and sinister particularity that gives his witches their emotional and theatrical power. Whether he is using historical sources or popular witchcraft pamphlets, he is able to transform the debates of his time into the ethical problems that his characters face as they move through a dramatic narrative. His readers and interpreters might use their knowledge of history to extend the imaginative range of their response to the characters and their story or they might, like Dr Johnson, use that knowledge to close off unacceptable readings of the play. The figure of the writer, however, stands before his readers' assimilation of the work into its history.

5

The Writer at Work

So far, in our discussion of 'the work', the writer, William Shakespeare, has been glimpsed only intermittently. His name has been invoked from time to time as the source of particular literary and poetic effects; he has been credited with making choices from Holinshed's chronicle that will inform the construction of his narrative and it has been suggested that the witches' speeches found in the Folio text, though possibly the work of another writer, might have been the result of a particularly creative reaction to the image in the frontispiece of *Newes from Scotland*.

The evidence for these connections is, of course, purely circumstantial. The sources that Shakespeare used, the process of composition and, above all, his views about his work have all to be inferred after the fact, working outwards from the text to historical circumstances in order to propose an invented personality that will offer a plausible author for the work as we know it.

The mixture of admiration, invention and speculation that attends all efforts to understand the connection between the writer and his work, are given enormous scope because of the gap that exists between the records of Shakespeare's life and the works that he produced. The records consist of raw information: his baptism on 26 April 1564, the license for his marriage to Anne Hathaway issued on November 27 1582 when Shakespeare was nineteen and his bride eight years his senior; the birth of his children: Susanna, baptized on 26 May 1583 (six months after her parents' wedding) and the twins, Hamnet and Judith, baptized on 2 February 1585. In 1597, Shakespeare bought New Place, the second largest dwelling in Stratford and he continued to deal in property and land with his Stratford fellows until he made his will in March 1616 and was buried on April 25 of the same year.[1]

Records of his life in London are similarly concerned with the details of his professional life. He was payee for performances at court before Queen Elizabeth by the Chamberlain's Men and, later, before James VI and I by the King's Men. He and his fellows in the Kings Men were awarded livery cloth to march in the King's coronation procession. He was a tenant of the Globe theatre and had shares in both that theatre and the Blackfriars playhouse; he lived in three locations in London, including the household of a Huguenot family.

There is evidence that during his playwriting career, Shakespeare attracted the attention of other writers. Famously, the pamphlet writer Robert Greene, or someone impersonating him,[2] warned against 'an upstart crow, beautified with our feathers... [who] is in his own conceit the onely Shake-scene in a country'[3] while others praised his 'honey-tongued' poetry, his excellence in comedy and tragedy and 'his right happy and copious industry'.[4]

None of the extant documents connect Shakespeare to *Macbeth*. Later biographers' attempts to make such connections often reveal more about their own model of a writer and his work than they do about this particular writer and how his work was made. For example, the great early nineteenth century scholar, Edmund Malone, devoted his working life to collecting documents about Shakespeare and exposing the fraudulent and fantastical myths that had grown up around him. However upon hearing a rumour that a letter from Shakespeare to the Earl of Dorset might have survived, he tempered his characteristic scepticism and wrote:

> I am... strongly inclined to think, that these letters, if indeed they exist, and are dated in 1606, or about that time, will turn out letters of thanks to the Treasurer, for some bounty transmitted through his hands by King James, in return for the tragedy of *Macbeth*.[5]

No such letters were ever discovered but Malone's fantasy about what they might have revealed shows how firmly the connection between *Macbeth* and King James had informed his assumptions about *Macbeth* and Shakespeare. A critical suggestion made by Dr Johnson, to defend the play's treatment of witches, had become a fact and the biographer was looking for documents that might corroborate it. No such document could, of course, exist since payments for playing, usually at a standard rate of £10, were made by the Revels Office to the playing company and not the author. The king's bounty was occasionally noted in the records for those payments, but the sums involved usually added up to the standard £10.[6]

Malone's model of an author whose creativity was personally rewarded by the king was derived from a romantic idea about the role of writers at the Renaissance court that owed more to the historical novels of Walter Scott than to early-modern theatre practice.[7] Both Scott and Malone were over-reading and taking literally the formula used in the prefatory matter of the 1623 Folio when it referred to the 'favour' that the 'Incomparable pair of Brethren', the Earls of Pembroke and Montgomery had shown the 'Author' of the plays. That prefatory matter, though very similar in its preface to the reader and dedicatory verses to the prefatory matter of other dramatic folios, has been read and re-read for all the clues it might offer about Shakespeare's reputation and the personal relationships that might have informed his work. In gathering together the works of William Shakespeare 'as he conceived them', the compilers of the Folio were not only concerned to turn a play into a work; they were also in the process of creating an author out of a playwright and the information they gave in doing so allowed subsequent generations to make the author they needed to fit their conceptions of the works.

In Heminges and Condell's preface, the author 'conceived' the work, he did not make it, and the metaphorical account of the process of writing continued in their assertions that

> His mind and hand went together, and what he thought, he uttered with that easiness that we have scarce received from him a blot in his papers.[8]

Heminges and Condell's suggested model for Shakespeare's creativity was one in which the content of the author's mind was transferred 'with…easiness' to his hand, with a pun on the physical hand and 'handwriting'. The play*wright* was no longer a maker, like a wheel*wright* or a cart*wright*, he was an author, the sole source of the work that he had conceived.

This model of artistic creativity was new in Shakespeare's time but subsequent discussions of Shakespeare that focused on the Folio made it commonplace and it certainly informs most modern biographers of Shakespeare. They find the mind of their creator in the plays and look for the sources of that creative mind in the connections they forge between the plays and the world that the author inhabited. The resulting research has often provided fascinating information about early modern culture but a model of creativity that assumes a direct instrumental relationship between the writer's life experience and his creative work often extends the connection between that information and the author.

For example, Michael Wood's enormously influential television and print biography, *In Search of Shakespeare*, uses his extensive research into the sources of Shakespeare's plays and the details of the world he inhabited to create a picture of the early-modern period. He connects that picture to Shakespeare in ways that offer a persuasive account of how this material might have entered Shakespeare's mind but says little about how it might have been transformed into the plays that he wrote:

> So, like any professional writer, Shakespeare was a sponge: stories of the street, things he saw, people he met, news of the day, sermons and tracts, all went into the mix. But he was a voracious reader, too, and books played their part.[9]

Wood's Shakespeare is modelled on the eclectic modern intellectual for whom ideas and events are grist to the mill of creativity and the creative work is fully the product of the author's mind. His Shakespeare had 'certainly read Southwell' (the Catholic poet and martyr) and Shakespeare's image in *Macbeth* of 'pity like a naked new born babe' that so puzzlingly ends with 'tears shall drown the wind' (1.7.21) is said to 'echo the surreal imagery of Southwell's poem "The Burning Babe"'. Southwell's poem, of course, uses the image rather differently. His babe sheds the tears himself while Shakespeare's are tears that 'drown the wind' shed by the eyes that have had the 'horrid deed' of Duncan's murder blown into them. However, Michael Wood only claims an 'echo', not a copy. The writer transforms his material and so it is impossible to pin his art down to a matter of positivist information or firm historical conclusions. Wood's Shakespeare also apparently

> read the work of the great Protestant preacher Henry Smith, published in 1593 by his friend Richard Field. Southwell and Field make a fascinating pair of complementary literary influences: from opposing sides doctrinally, both write about power and conscience and both are literary models of great power...the debate about the nature of the poet involved everyone, from all walks of life and across the whole spectrum of religious belief.[10]

In Wood's biography, and many others, a similarity of imagery between a Shakespeare text and a Catholic poet, a connection between Shakespeare and a printer from Stratford, an extrapolation from doctrinally complex works of theology to the abstract themes of 'power' and 'conscience' are combined to create an immensely attractive image of an author who is open to all experience and whose life and plays will together provide easy access to a fascinating, but ultimately familiar, world. The plays of Shakespeare have provided generations of readers and audiences with an image of the early modern period that stands in the way of an independent assessment of its nature.

This emphasis on the writer as both the creator of the work and as our route into his world is echoed in Stephen Greenblatt's biography, *Will in the World*.[11] Greenblatt is content to acknowledge the 'huge gaps in knowledge that make any biographical study of Shakespeare an exercise in speculation' but is also willing to draw on what he calls the 'dogged archival labour' of the 'eager scholars' who have provided him and other biographers with the records that ground his subject in the life-world of early modern England. These earlier scholars scoured the literature of early modern England to identify the possible sources of and analogues to Shakespeare's plays; later biographers turn these connections into stories, which together make up a plausible and satisfying version of the world of Shakespeare.

In his magisterial compendium of the *Narrative and Dramatic Sources of Shakespeare*, Geoffrey Bullough recorded a pageant presented to King James VI and I at Oxford in 1605 in which three sibyls told a story of Banquo meeting 'fatal Sisters' who prophesied that he would have 'power without end'. They then turned to the king and greeted him with

Hail, whom Scotland serves!
Whom England, hail!
Whom Ireland serves, all hail.[12]

Bullough cites the pageant as no more than an analogue to Shakespeare's play, but for the biographer, the repeated 'all hails' resonate too strongly with *Macbeth* to avoid filling in the 'huge gaps'. The writer of the pageant presented at St John's College and Shakespeare could independently have been using Holinshed, the obvious source for knowledge about Scotland but the possibility of a connection between Shakespeare and a royal performance is too tempting to be avoided.

Greenblatt's narrative is scrupulously conditional: '*If* he were anywhere near Oxford at the time, Shakespeare *would have had* the strongest professional reason to see how the performances were received'[13] (though since he had no connection with St John's College or the royal court, there is no reason why he would have been invited). Nevertheless the traditional connection between King James and *Macbeth* is strong enough to become part of a substantive narrative. According to Greenblatt, when the king of Denmark visited the court in 1606,

> It was probably on one of these festive occasions that James sat down with his guests to see *Macbeth*...Shakespeare must have seen, or heard about, those three boys dressed up as ancient sibyls, and he had not forgotten them. He conjured them up in *Macbeth* to restage the reassuring vision of unbroken dynastic succession.[14]

The art of the biographer allows an elegant movement from the historical or literary record to the writer's experience. Familiar critical ideas about the play are then used to show how those experiences might have entered the playwright's consciousness and imagination. The writer who emerges from those connections is an all-seeing artist whose plays provide a privileged access to the alien country of the past.

In the hands of biographers *Macbeth* is 'constructed around, or perhaps as, a piece of flattery'. However, the image of the writer as mere flatterer cannot be allowed to stand, so the larger national crisis of the Gunpowder plot is brought to bear on the connection between the writer, the work and the times:

> In Macbeth, Shakespeare seems to have set out to write a play that would function as a collective ritual of reassurance...The staging of

the events of eleventh century Scotland...allowed its seventeenth century audience to face a symbolic version of this disaster and to witness the triumphant restoration of order.[15]

Based on two scenes in *Macbeth*, the Porter monologue, and the parade of kings from Act 4, the writer has become a priestly healer of the nation. The fact that neither of these scenes are noticed by the only eye-witness of the play's performance and that Leeds Barroll has systematically undermined the connection between the play and the royal court[16] cannot be allowed to stand in the way of the modern readers' need for collective reassurance that a writer of genius (the biographer as much as Shakespeare) can be made to retell the larger truth about history. In this version of the writer and his work, the writer of genius writes a work for and on behalf of the king and the nation. The fact that no contemporary seems to have noticed the connection, is overshadowed by the evidence that the work itself can provide when interpreted by a skilled biographer.

THE WORK OF WRITING

These engaging and plausible accounts of Shakespeare's life as a creative artist offer suggestive versions of the myriad sources that Shakespeare might have been exposed to in his life experience, his wide reading, his relations with players and his connection to the court entertainment bureaucracy. They construct a writer who we can understand and sympathize with and a work whose puzzles and complexity have been turned into resonant moral themes of power and conscience or significant moments that connect with the legendary crises of early modern politics.

By engaging the reader of biography and theatre history, these accounts encourage an imaginative empathy with the work but they leave completely unanswered the question of how the work was written, how the writer might have moved through the moment by moment experience of making a five act play that turns narrative into dramatic action and explanation into poetry. The romantic assumption that literary effects of narrative and character flow spontaneously from the author's genius, allows readers and audiences to respond with generalized admiration to the work's effects. It cannot explain, in detail, how this writer, whose life experience and working relationships were far from unique, produced this play.

When we place *Macbeth* in the context of Shakespeare's earlier plays, however, it is possible to see the writer making a number of technical changes that together provide an insight into the sources of its literary and theatrical power. By the time Shakespeare was writing *Macbeth*, he had the history plays under his belt. In choosing a narrative of regicide for *Macbeth*, Shakespeare was returning to writing a play with characters who contemplate murder and deal with the act itself and with its psychic and ethical consequences. Echoes of those earlier treatments are to be found throughout *Macbeth* and they provide some sense of how Shakespeare worked through similar dramatic situations to create different effects.

The justly famous scene in which Macbeth and his lady quarrel over Macbeth's failure of resolve, for example, builds on a similar scene from *Richard III* where two nameless murderers argue about their task of killing Clarence, the brother who stands in the way of Richard's ascent to the throne. The murderers in *Richard III* are generic figures: they never appear again and their dialogue about conscience is a set piece. It fills out the scene and offers the local pleasure of a counter-ethical rhetorical argument like those that were set for Elizabethan schoolboys and law students. The first murderer goes through the rhetorical arguments against the force of conscience:

> It makes a man a coward. A man cannot steal but it accuseth him. A man cannot swear but it checks him. A man cannot lie with his neighbour's wife but it detects him. 'Tis a blushing shamefaced spirit, that mutinies in a man's bosom. It fills a man full of obstacles. It made me once restore a purse of gold that by chance I found. It beggars any man that keeps it. It is turned out of towns and cities for a dangerous thing, and every man that means to live well endeavours to trust to himself and live without it. (*Richard III*, 1.4.127–35)[17]

By turning conventional ideas about conscience on their head, Shakespeare gives the murderers a sense of individuality that then informs their moving exchange with Clarence when he wakes and remembers his traumatic dream of murdering Rutland.

The scene moves rather slowly from set speech to set speech but it shows the writer's early efforts to create the sense of a character's inner life by linking action to memory and the ethical choices that the narrative offers. It opens up the possibility of demonstrating, however comically, the murderers' potential for pity and the long ensuing argument between them and Clarence that elaborates the deep political and ethical questions of an individual's contested allegiance to monarch, kin and God.

When Macbeth and his lady engage in a similar debate about conscience, the tension in the scene is of course far greater. The gap between conscience and self-interest that creates the rhetorical opposition in the murderers' speeches from *Richard III*, is not in *Macbeth* explicitly argued for. Its ethical reality and psychic cost have instead been dramatized in Lady Macbeth's appeal to the spirits that tend on mortal thoughts and Macbeth's vision of the dagger and his agonized wish that 'it were done when 'tis done'. These characters' contemplation of murderous self-interest is elaborated through images that range across the natural and supernatural world to create characters whose lives seem to extend beyond the action of the play and whose fear and anger have a psychic as well as an ethical credibility.

The later play absorbs the murderers into the main action. It is also more closely connected to the narrative by the explicit reference to Duncan's off-stage feast and the connection between Macbeth's speech about conscience and the urgent narrative sense of a deed waiting to be done. However, the shared deep structure of both scenes, a long speech on conscience followed by an argument, is still visible in the later play. As we have seen, (above 24–6) Macbeth's conscience speech is driven by images that do not connect logically and so seems to offer insight into the confusion engendered by his unique trauma. In *Richard III*, Clarence's murderer takes his argument more slowly but deals in similar paradoxes. When his companion asks, 'What, art thou afraid', he responds, 'Not to kill him, having a warrant, but to be damned for killing him, from which no warrant can defend me' (1.4.105–7). The confusion between secular and religious authority is an obvious logical fault and it links the murderer's speech to the clown dialogues that used similar devices in Shakespeare's early comedies. The murderer's comic confusion between a warrant from the king and the absolute demands of religion are, in *Macbeth*, compressed and reanimated in the alliterative, visual image of angels pleading 'trumpet-tongued against the deep-damnation of his taking off' (1.7.19–20).

In the earlier history plays, Shakespeare often uses rhetorical exercises to develop a scene or to complicate a character but as his style develops we also find him adapting conventional metaphors, refining commonplace ideas and turning them into visual images that creates a startling sense of a spontaneous and idiosyncratic expression of feeling. In the third act of *2 Henry IV*, for example, the exhausted, demoralized king reflects on his inability to sleep:

> O sleep, O gentle sleep,
> Nature's soft nurse, how have I frighted thee,
> That thou no more wilt weigh my eyelids down
> And steep my senses in forgetfulness.

> (3.1.6–9)

The speech takes its time and makes its devices obvious as it moves from the idea of sleep, adds an adjective that humanizes it, 'gentle sleep', and then, in the second line, turns it into a full blown personification 'Nature's soft nurse'. It continues into one of Shakespeare's famous set pieces that expatiates on the familiar (if disputable) idea that kings sleep worse than common folk, with an extraordinary description of sleeping commoners, including the exhausted ship-boy asleep 'upon the high and giddy mast' of a ship in a storm.

This extension of poetic commonplace into vivid description was one of Shakespeare's great strengths from the earliest stages of his career. However, from quite early in his career, in *Love's Labours Lost* and in the 'Pyramus and Thisbe' play at the end of *A Midsummer's Night's Dream* he began to mock and satirize the dangers of rhetorical elaboration in Holofernes' pedantic displays of learning and Bottom's parody of his own style:

> O grim-looked night! O night with hue so black!
> O night, which ever art when day is not!
> O night, O night, alack, alack, alack,
> I fear my Thisbe's promise is forgot.

> (5.1.168–71)

So, when the commonplace ideas about sleep are built into Macbeth's speech, they become much more compressed and the elaboration of the image comes to seem part of the speaker's psychological situation rather than a poetic device.

When he returns from murdering Duncan, Macbeth tells his lady 'Methought I heard a voice cry, "Sleep no more: / *Macbeth* does murder sleep" '. He then seems unable to leave the idea alone,

> the innocent sleep,
> Sleep that knits up the ravelld sleeve of care,
> The death of each days life, sore labours bath,
> Balm of hurt minds, great natures second course,
> Chief nourisher in life's feast.

> (2.2.43–7)

These lines have been so often anthologized that they have come to seem a particularly resonant evocation of a universal experience. However, they are also a list of commonplaces, a kind of poet's manual of the ways in which sleep can be described. Their impact in the play depends on the way that Shakespeare links poetry to action, tying the poetry back to the situation of the murder and Macbeth's reaction to it. The lines are no longer primarily a statement about sleep but a dramatic exemplar of a character's crazed, obsessive, turning over of an idea, turning his mind away from the horror of the murder scene to more manageable thoughts. The dramatic, rather than the poetic role of the idea about sleep is then reinforced by Macbeth's lady's response: 'What do you mean?' Shakespeare boldly indicates that these ideas about sleep are beside the point: elegant commonplace is pushed aside in order to focus on the dramatic relationship between the characters.

Throughout *Macbeth*, poetry is subordinated to narrative and character. Shakespeare moves from commonplace ideas about the world to a point of view that seems forced from his characters in extreme situations and so entirely spontaneous. Comparison with *2 Henry IV* illustrates the point. In the same scene as the speech about sleep, King Henry goes into another set-piece about the impossibility of seeing the future. The prologue to this is an exchange with his nobles about 'the body of our kingdom/How foul it is, what rank diseases grow,/And with what danger at the heart of it'. Again the idea is familiar

enough for Henry's courtier, Warwick, to take up the metaphor
and carry it on into his reply:

> It is but as a body yet distempered,
> Which to his former strength may be restored
> With good advice and little medicine

(3.1.38–43)

In *Macbeth*, by contrast, the almost dead metaphor of the
country as a body is suddenly brought to life with the tiny
exchange between Macbeth and the doctor who reports on Lady
Macbeth's illness. Their exchange is not a free standing set-piece
but is inserted into a scene full of action in which Macbeth arms
to respond to the news of Birnam wood's march to Dunsinane.
The image of the diseased country comes as Macbeth dismisses
the doctor, bickers with Seyton and ends with the wish that his
English enemies could be dispatched with a laxative. When the
doctor says that he cannot cure Lady Macbeth's mental state,
Macbeth responds

> Throw physic to the dogs, I'll none of it. –
> Come, put mine armour on; give me my staff. –
> Seyton, send out. – Doctor, the thanes fly from me. –
> Come sir, dispatch. – If thou could'st, doctor, cast
> The water of my land, find her disease,
> And purge it to a sound and pristine health,
> I would applaud thee to the very echo
> That should applaud again. – Pull't off I say! –
> What rhubarb, cynne, or what purgative drug
> Would scour these English hence?

(5.3.48–57)

His final challenge to the doctor is an aggressive question about
how much he knows of the English invasion – 'Hear'st thou of
them' – which makes the doctor, in spite of his diplomatic
answer, fear for his future. The exchange dramatizes Macbeth's
emotional state and the situation of all those trapped in the
besieged castle with him. Metaphor has been turned into drama
and the generalized ideas about the connection between the
state and the human body have been given a dynamic dramatic
resonance.

These echoes of Shakespeare's history plays in *Macbeth*, create
a sense of a writer working at his craft of turning rhetoric and

85

poetry into poetic drama. Poetic commonplaces about the nature of sleep or the metaphors of the commonwealth as a body are pressed back into the construction of characters responding to particular situations. The history plays also provided Shakespeare with scope in which to explore ways of generating an emotional response to the larger action of dynastic struggles and national affairs. In both *Richard III* and *King John* he explored the impact of suffering children in creating an emotional structure of feeling that ran alongside the political issues addressed in the plays.

In *King John*, for example, the murder of Prince Arthur is given an extended sequence where the little prince pleads with Hubert, suborned to kill him at King John's request. The scene fulfils a number of narrative and dramatic functions. It creates localized emotion as little Arthur is unknowingly affectionate towards his murderer and then vividly expresses his horror at the prospect of having his eyes put out by contrasting that pain with the agony of having that even 'a mote ... a grain a dust, a gnat, a wandering hair' (4.1.91–2) in his eyes. Arthur's pleading makes Hubert draw back from murdering him. This action allows a further twist in the plot where King John refuses to reward Hubert and, since Arthur is still alive makes room for a further scene of pathos in which Arthur is killed escaping over the wall of his prison.

In *Richard III* Shakespeare has a different take on the death of children. There the princes are presented before their death, engaged in witty and pointed banter with their uncle (3.1.). Their death is not shown on stage but instead described in a sentimental set-piece (4.3.1–22). The location of this speech allows it to act as the tilting point of the play's action as Tirrel's depiction of the princes' death is followed by news of growing resistance to King Richard. The connection between Richard's political difficulties and his villainous murder of the children is made again in the following scene where the lamenting queens whose sons have all been murdered present a chorus of grief that brings together the play's historical trajectory and the immediate, experienced sorrow of its particular events (4.4.39–60).

In *Macbeth* Shakespeare reworks that structural use of pathos generated by the death of children to similar effect. Macduff's young son is given a prattling exchange with his mother that is both, like Arthur's exchange with Hubert, a pathetic attempt to comfort her and, like the princes in *Richard III*, a tellingly cynical observation on the power of 'liars and swearers' over honest men. In the scene where Macduff receives the news of his family's destruction, Shakespeare avoids the temptation to offer a speech of lengthy lamentation. He engages the audience's imaginative empathy with his character by implying, rather than expressing, emotion in Macduff's agonized and eloquent silence. In *Richard III* and *King John* we can see an affecting, slow-motion connection being made between large historical patterns and the suffering of individuals. In *Macbeth*, the process is much more compressed and the emotion is tightly tied to the dramatic situation of individual characters. As a result, the characters invite empathy with them as individuals and that empathy is separated out from ethical considerations.

In *Richard III* Shakespeare experimented with ways of creating empathy with a character whose actions are entirely reprehensible. Judgements about his immoral and instrumental treatment of Lady Anne or his cavalier treachery towards his supporters are constantly mitigated by Richard's engagement with the audience through his self-mocking soliloquies (see 1.2.215–50) or his witty refusal to engage with his victims' distress (see 4.3. for Richard's treatment of Buckingham). At the end of the play, after Richard has been confronted by the ghosts of his victims, his conscience-stricken terror is displayed by separating his character into two parts as he contemplates his sins and their effect, unseen until now, on his personality:

> Cold fearful drops stand on my trembling flesh.
> What do I fear? Myself? There's none else by.
> Richard loves Richard: that is, I am I
> Is there a murderer here? No. Yes, I am,
> Then fly! What, from myself? Great reason. Why?
> Lest I revenge. Myself upon myself?
> Alack, I love myself. Wherefore? For any good
> That I myself have done unto myself?
> O no, alas, I rather hate myself
> For hateful deeds committed by myself.

(5.5.135–44)

This slightly clumsy conflation of the two sides of an ethical debate has, by the time Shakespeare is writing *Macbeth*, been turned into a single consistent presentation of a character who understands the evil he is about to commit and who can contemplate its impact in eloquent poetry.

Shakespeare dramatizes Macbeth as a man who experiences a visceral, physical awareness of evil. He is not frightened of the witches on their first encounter but the contemplated deed is one 'Whose horrid image doth unfix my hair,/And make my seated heart knock at my ribs,/Against the use of nature?' (1.3.135–7). He feels the evil on his body and the play reiterates that sense of bodily experience as a way into the emotions. After he has ascended the throne Macbeth speaks to his lady of 'the affliction of these terrible dreams/That shake us nightly' (3.2.20–1) and conjures up the extraordinary image of paranoia in a mind 'full of scorpions' (3.2.39). In the final act, as the English troops approach, his psychological state is dramatized in his violent swings from rage at the unfortunate messenger in 5.3 to the elegiac contemplation of his empty life bereft of 'honour, love, obedience, troops of friends' (5.3.25) or the justly famous comparison of his life to the 'walking shadow' that 'struts and frets his hour upon the stage,/And then is heard no more' (5.5.17–27). Shakespeare could have encountered these ways of relating physical to emotional awareness in the growing number of published discussions of the scientific and the psychic make-up of human beings.[18] However, the craft with which he turned those ideas into theatre owed a significant amount to his own experiments in reconfiguring the relationship between narrative and character, events and emotion.

The most telling success in these experiments came in the development of Macbeth's lady. In both *Richard III* and *King John*, much of the emotion is generated by lamenting queens whose elegiac speeches sum up the historical action of the plays in litanies of murder and betrayal. In those speeches they continually present themselves as wives and mothers, betrayed by the murderous actions of men. They present themselves, too, as victims of dynastic struggles, turning the complex politics of the Wars of the Roses into generalized emotions about the loss of sons and husbands on both sides.

Richard III varies this pattern in the creation of Queen Margaret, widow of the murdered King Henry VI. Her initial action in the play is to gather up its preceding events in a mighty curse against her enemies ranged on the stage. Her presence on the stage is extremely powerful, first commenting from the side-lines on the wrangling among those who are now in power, and then exploding into an extended imprecation on each in turn, matching their former ills done to her with prophetic wishes for their future destruction. Given the impact of this performance, it is surprising that Queen Margaret does not reappear for another two acts. Her curses are all related to the fate of her family and when she returns, it is to lament with the other queens who have suffered as she predicted they would. The queens' lament, with its reiterated mourning for those destroyed by men is a choric summary of the events to date. It presents the women making common cause in their grieving witness. Margaret initially triumphs over her former enemies but the Duchess of York prays

> O Harry's wife, triumph not in my woes
> God witness with me, I have wept for thine.

> (4.4.59–60)

Queen Margaret responds with a summary of the situation of all the women in the play:

> I called thee then 'vain flourish of my fortune';
> I called thee then, poor shadow, 'painted queen'
> The presentation of but what I was,
> The flattering index of a direful pageant,
> Once heaved a-high to be hurled down below.
> A mother only mocked with two fair babes,
> A dream of what thou wast, a garish flag
> To be the aim of every dangerous shot,
> A sign of dignity, a breath, a bubble,
> A queen in jest, only to fill the scene.

> (4.4.82–91)

The sad litany is built up from a list, turned into end-stopped poetic images. Queen Margaret, for all her historic and histrionic power becomes a chorus to the main event. This historical presentation of a powerful woman, laid low by the actions of men, lies behind Shakespeare's creation of Lady Macbeth and is a measure of his achievement in the construction of a different kind of female figure.

Lady Macbeth, famously, has no children. She is an active participant in Duncan's murder and when she does lament the deaths that her husband has caused, the words are forced out of her in fragments of prose as she walks in her sleep. The poetic pleasures of eloquent elegy are turned into a new, but equally powerful, representation of the psychic consequences of evil deeds she has witnessed. Moreover, Shakespeare's innovation was remarked on by Simon Forman: 'Observe also howe Mackbetes quen did rise in the night in her slepe, & walke and talked and confessed all, and the doctor noted her wordes'.[19]

Shakespeare's creative work in adapting motifs from his own history plays involved pressing his facility in extended poetic and rhetorical set-pieces back into character and situation. The history plays' separation between the politics (for men) and emotional lament (for women)[20] was reconfigured into the creation of psychically complex characters. Their poetic arias worked through the juxtaposition of disparate images that implied rather than elaborating the emotional and ethical implications of their actions and the effect was to demand a kind of attention from the audience that worked through empathy as much as judgement.

In spite of these differences in effect, *Macbeth* is nonetheless linked to Shakespeare's history plays in the shared project of turning narratives of events into a locus of complex emotional response. In the play's final scenes, the intense focus on Macbeth and his lady gives way to alternating scenes that chart the progression of the English invasion. There the lessons of the history plays are more in evidence; lessons in how to manage and pace a battle scene and how to create the emotional charge needed if the drum and trumpet of staged warfare was to result in an affecting narrative.

In one of Shakespeare's earliest history plays, *1 Henry VI* the role of heroic manhood is given to Talbot, a legendary figure who displays the wit and gracious chivalry, as well as the prowess, expected of an English hero. Shakespeare's version of this figure is given an additional emotional dimension by the appearance of his son, John, whom Talbot has not seen for seven years. They first encounter one another in battle and they resolve to fight together. Talbot is then shown rescuing his son from the French soldiers and, after the battle, recounts how his son saved him. This heroic companionship between father and son is given its full emotional power when John's body is brought to Talbot after the fight. Talbot laments his death and dies with his dead son in his arms.

In *Macbeth*, Shakespeare draws on these values of heroic manhood to denigrate Macbeth's forces and by introducing a son for Siward, Malcolm's companion in the Scottish invasion, he creates both an emotional focus for the English forces and an addition to the drama leading up to the final encounter between Macbeth and Macduff. Siward's son, in his only speaking moment in the play, encounters Macbeth in the heat of battle. He bravely stands up to him in the verbal confrontation that precedes their fight but Macbeth overcomes him. The stage direction *'Fight and young Siward slain'* leaves open different possibilities for the nature of the fight. It need not endorse Macbeth's conclusion 'Thou wast born of woman' (5.7.12), by making Macbeth's victory an easy one, for the fight has both to emphasize Young Siward's heroism and act as a suspense-filled prelude to the finale.

When Young Siward's death is announced, his father responds according to the values of chivalric heroism. He asks 'Had he his hurts before?', that is, gained fighting, not retreating. He is assured that they were 'on the front' and concludes 'Why then, God's soldier be he' (5.9.12–14). The simple tenets of heroism, complicated and compromised in the history plays, are here simply invoked to establish a counter-vailing set of values to the power of the defeated Macbeth.

In his selection, for *Macbeth*, from his own history plays, Shakespeare compressed his earlier tendency to rhetorical elaboration and, for the most part, tightened the focus on motifs and dramatic situations that would move forward the narrative and create the complex relationships among his characters. In working with other sources, Shakespeare seems to have followed a similar creative trajectory. As we have seen, in writing the history of Macbeth, he understandably took up the long English tradition of historical writing in which Macbeth was presented as a bloody tyrant, necessarily brought under English rule with the help of the lords who controlled the shifting and contested border country of the north. There was another tradition, heard in the praise songs for Macbeth of the flaming hair, the provider of food and safety in the way of pre-feudal warrior kings.[21] Shakespeare either did not know or chose to ignore those ancient stories because they could not inform the structure of the story that he told.

In the case of Macbeth's lady, however, the ancient story of the warrior peoples around the nation of England may have lain beneath the complex human personality that emerged from the play's dramatic structure. In the stories of English conflict with its bordering nations, their wild and unseemly nature was emphasized by the presence of fierce women in their forces. In the opening scene of *I Henry IV*, Westmorland tells the king of his cousin Mortimer's defeat by the Welsh forces. In the course of the battle there were

> A thousand of his people butchered,
> Upon whose dead corpse there was such misuse,
> Such beastly shameless transformation
> By those Welshwomen done, as may not be
> Without much shame retold or spoken of.

(1.1.42–6)

The 'shameless transformation' that Shakespeare forbore to speak of is more clearly noted in Holinshed's account of the cruelty of another foreign queen, the Sycthian Tomyzis. Her actions are compared to those of Welshwomen who defaced their enemies' bodies by stuffing their penises into their mouths. This violation is described by Holinshed as 'to the shame of a sex pretending the title of weake vessels'. This inhuman as well as unwomanly action is used to characterize the foreignness of England's enemies who are repeatedly defined as the opposite of the manly and heroic English. Holinshed's presentation of the Scottish women warriors includes a grudging admiration for their bravery:

> In these daies also the women of our countrie were of no less courage than the men, for all stout maidens and wives (if they were not with child) marched well in the field as did the men, and so soone as the armie did set forward, they slue the first living creature that they found, in whose blood they not onlie bathed their swords, but also tasted thereof with their mouthes.[22]

These heroic women were also praised as mothers:

Each woman would also take intolerable pains to bring up and nourish her own children. They thought them furthermore not to be kindly, except they were so well nourished after their births with the milk of their breasts as they were before they were born with the blood of their own bellies: nay they feared lest they should degenerate and grow out of kind, except they gave them such themselves.[23]

Breastfeeding women were seen as the antithesis of aristocratic English women who, for the most part, sent their children out to nurse but that antithesis also included elements of primitive purity as well as barbarism.

These passages offer a number of ideas of womanhood that hold in tension purity, heroism and barbarism. A (literal) taste for blood is connected to the blood that nourishes Scottish infants in the womb and is transformed into the mothers' milk that will ensure the children's future heroic qualities. The almost magical quality of women to partake in the change of humours from blood to milk lies behind Lady Macbeth's call to the spirits to unsex her. The same complex of ideas is compressed into Lady Macbeth's famous and passionate articulation of the power of her promises:

> I have given suck and know
> How tender 'tis to love the babe that milks me:
> I would, while it was smiling in my face,
> Have plucked the nipple from his boneless gums
> And dashed the brains out, had I so sworn
> As you have done to this.

> (1.7.54–9)

The speech, as dramatized, seems to come spontaneously from her experience: there is no rhetorical elaboration of a comparison with Scottish warriors, or classical queens. Its startling directness has caused critical problems since it is not corroborated elsewhere in the play either in the lady's actions or in other references to her children. However, it is a particularly striking example of Shakespeare's working method in this play: his ability to work through a complex of contemporary ideas taken from his literary sources into a powerful poetic image that animates a local theatrical effect.

The contradictions within these ideas, perhaps more so than a pre-existing notion of a coherent individual, are brought together in different episodes in the play. Together they create the illusion of complex characterization, of a created personality who emerges and changes under pressure from the events in which she is entangled. Passages from Shakespeare's reading, ideas from his culture, episodes and dramatic techniques that he used elsewhere are *worked on* (this is the writer at work) to create poetic drama whose resonances extend beyond the moment of its creation through the further work of readers, audiences and commentators.

6

The Work Reworked

Shakespeare's creative work in adapting the images and structures of the history plays into the psychic and emotional experience of *Macbeth* shows his developing skill as a dramatist, converting narrative and history into characters whose poetic articulation of their dramatic situation offers potential for an audience's empathetic engagement. He used these recurring motifs to create structures of feeling that articulated and, in a sense created, the terms with which to deal with extreme states of emotion. Our modern sense of the traumatic consequences of evil actions in psychic breakdown, suicide and self-destruction is in part enabled by Shakespeare's achievement in placing the political and ethical frameworks of judgement in tension with emotion and empathy. This tension between judgement and empathy, together with a concern to find a definable significance for the play's meaning in its historical frame, has been at the heart of subsequent treatment of the play and has generated the terms of its reception in both the theatre and in criticism.

The achievement involved in creating those complex literary and dramatic effects has, for the most part, been attributed to the creative artistry of the writer. Whether flattering the king, or engaging in a 'collective ritual of reassurance', or even reworking his own earlier style, the writer is usually presented as co-extensive with the work – and in some cases the one substitutes for the other: 'Shakespeare' means both the writer and his work.

This view of Shakespeare as a god-like figure who created a world from nothing[1] has inevitably been resisted. From the mid-twentieth century, literary theorists questioned the idea of an author as the sole source of artistic effect or the work of art as the seamless creation of a single mind. In the case of Shakespeare, that critical tendency against the romantic view of authorship was linked with a view that insisted on Shakespeare's role as a man of the theatre, a sharer in a playing company, an actor and entrepreneur who was alert to the commercial implications of his work and wrote in collaboration with others.

There is, of course, ample primary evidence for this aspect of Shakespeare's life: his name crops up in the records of his playing company and in the bequests of players' wills,[2] and part of the praise for his 'work' in the commendatory verses to the second edition of the Folio gave him credit for keeping the theatres open, even after his death:

> But O! what praise more powerful can we give
> The dead than that by him the King's Men live,
> His players, which should they but have shared the fate
> All else expired within the short term's date,
> How could the Globe have prospered, since through want
> Of change the plays and poems had grown scant.[3]

This praise for Shakespeare as a man of theatre was written before 1632 when the debate about theatrical taste was at its height, but, along with the commendatory prefaces and verses to the First Folio, it began the association of Shakespeare's continuing significance as a writer with the success of the stage.

The story of Shakespeare the theatre practitioner was as subject to myth-making as any of the other connections between the writer and his work. Some critics used it to excuse Shakespeare from what they regarded as lapses in taste imposed on him by the needs of a vulgar audience. Others have presented it as an iconoclastic move, reducing the writer of genius to a mere hack, motivated by opportunistic commercialism. A more systematic analysis of the development of Shakespeare's playing company has suggested that the company's developing repertory and that of their competitor companies may have been as much of a motivating and determining force in Shakespeare's creative output as any particular life-events or changes in the world of politics and the court.

Roslyn Knutson's work on *The Repertory of Shakespeare's Company* has identified a pattern of playing in which the different companies' plays tended to cluster thematically, with a successful play in one company being picked up by a new play, with a similar story in another.

In most years the Admiral's Men (a rival company) offered plays on stories from the history of ancient Britain: for example, *Cutlack* in 1594–95, *Valteger* in 1596–97 and 1601–2, the two part *Brute* in 1598–99, and *Malcolm King of Scots* in 1601–2. The Chamberlain's and King's Men may have followed suit, but Shakespeare himself was not the supplier until 1605–6, when he wrote *Macbeth* and *King Lear*.

Knutson's work acts as a salutary reminder that the theatre was part of a growing entertainment industry in which the companies identified their market through their competitors as much as through the political issues of the times or the inspiration of particular writers. An interest in Scottish stories that biographers have connected with the accession of King James VI of Scotland to the throne of England, may equally have been generated by the more general sense that history plays had been a strong suit in the theatres for a decade.

Knutson's work has also emphasized the importance of revivals in developing a repertory that was a mix of old and new plays. Once again, Shakespeare's plays were included in the mix:

> In 1604–5, for example, in a year when *Othello* and *Measure for Measure* were new, at least five of his old works were also in production ... in 1610–11, when *The Winter's Tale* was new, *Cymbeline* and *Othello* were continued from 1609–10 and his *Macbeth* was being revived.[4]

The implications of a repertory approach are very significant indeed for understanding the writer and his work. They release the play from its purely topical connection to historical events, (such as the Gunpowder plot which would have been old news in 1611) and they allow for the possibility of seeing a play as part of a writer's working (rather than psychic or political) relationship to his time. That working relationship produced extraordinary innovation in matching dramatic narrative to poetry, it extended the range of dramatic writing in ways that were admired and imitated by contemporaries but it also built on the skills of performers and depended on the organization of players in a company.

This democratic sense of Shakespeare as a first among equals, a player in a company, has been taken up by theatre historians who emphasize the collaborative nature of early-modern theatre, pointing to the number of plays written by teams of writers, working in partnership with playing companies. We know that, towards the end of his writing career, Shakespeare collaborated on two plays, *The Two Noble Kinsmen* and *Henry VIII* with John Fletcher, the dramatist who succeeded him as a principal playwright for the King's Men. The relationship between Shakespeare and Middleton has also attracted significant attention and Middleton's role as a co-author in *Macbeth* has become a commonplace of modern commentary on the play.[5]

In judging the evidence for other authors' work in *Macbeth*, it is important to be clear about the nature of that evidence and to distinguish between the different implications of evidence taken from the history of the text, and the history of the theatre. As we have seen, when Simon Forman recorded his visit to the play in 1611, he made no mention of the witch scenes, apart from the opening prophecy, and nor did he remember the porter. It may be that those episodes that biographers have wished to link to James's accession were omitted in the later version for the stage. Alternatively, the fact that they were included in the Folio text could provide evidence of additions to the play made between 1611 when Forman saw it and 1623 when the Folio was published. What ever decision is made about the role and dating of different writers' interventions, this view of the text suggests a work that is less an organic work of art and more a loosely connected sequence of scenes built around the central narrative of regicide and revenge.

This idea of a more loosely structured and changeable text has been adopted by recent scholars of Shakespeare's text to suggest a distinction between the play in the theatre and the literary text saved for posterity by the Folio of 1623. *Macbeth* is the third shortest play in the Folio and the scholarly consensus is that the play 'suffered from posthumous theatrical adaptation'.[6] Textual scholars' keen awareness of the layers of activity that lie between an author's missing fair copy and the printed version, together with the gap in time between the presumed date of the play and its printing in the Folio, have led them to propose that the Folio text, in spite of Heminges and Condell's assurances, is based on a script adapted for the theatre.[7]

In Act 3, Scene 5 (the Hecate scene) and Act 4, Scene 1 (the cauldron scene) the Folio text includes instructions for songs, quoting only their first lines. Neither song is necessary for any narrative purpose and some readers have found the idea of Shakespeare's witches singing so antithetical to their roles as harbingers of evil that they conclude that the songs must have been added to the play at a later stage. Since full texts of the songs occur in the manuscript of Thomas Middleton's play, *The Witch*, it is concluded that Middleton must have inserted the songs into the text for performance and his additions have made their way – albeit only as first lines – into the Folio text. The whole scene in which these songs appear, also seems different in tone from the witches elsewhere, so the entire Hecate scene is granted to Middleton. The full text of the songs appeared in William Davenant's adaptation of *Macbeth* published in 1674, suggesting that these songs were part of a stage tradition. The idea that *Macbeth,* as preserved in the Folio collection, may be the trace of a porous and provisional theatrical production is entirely plausible. It fits what is known of theatre practice and it also suits with a post-modern view of literary works that allows them to be temporary, in process, created and recreated at different times for different purposes.

Nevertheless, the existence of two songs that also occur in the manuscript of another playwright is not in itself evidence of wholesale adaptation or a problematic relationship between a work and its writer. The transmission of songs could have gone in the other direction – Shakespeare to Middleton – or both writers could have taken the songs from a third source.[8] As William St Clair explains,

> Both Middleton and Shakespeare may have been using a song which had already been printed. Since the intellectual property regime applied only to texts that had been reified into printed books, a player could be scripted by a playwright to sing an existing song without having to obtain permission…By quoting a song in a manuscript, Middleton would not have breached intellectual property, but he might have run into problems if his manuscript of *The Witch* had ever proceeded to print.[9]

The connection between the songs in Macbeth and in Middleton, in other words, does not in itself demonstrate that the play as printed in the Folio is a product of collaboration. Evidence for Middleton's hand in the play is, however, reinforced by the evidence of stage directions that use the form '*enter* (character A) *meeting* (character B)'. This form of stage

99

direction occurs far more frequently in Middleton's plays than elsewhere and is used in *Macbeth* for 2.1. *'Enter King... meeting a bleeding Captain'* and for 3.5. *'Enter the three witches meeting Hecate'*.

The case for Middleton's role in the play, in other words, is made by the accumulation of detail, linked to a comprehensive knowledge of the characteristic styles of contemporary dramatists. Nevertheless, the impulse to claim collaboration is nearly always linked in the first instance to a sense of the fragmentary nature of the work itself. In the case of the collaboration with Middleton, the search for a collaborator arises, in part, from the ambiguous characters of the witch scenes and the continuing unease that they create. Act 3, Scene 5, in which the first song appears, comes just after the scene with Banquo's ghost that ends with Macbeth resolving to go again to the witches. The appearance of Hecate introduces a new witch into the story. Unlike the witches of 1.3, she is not a village witch who might be found killing swine or quarrelling with the 'rump-fed runyon': she is the classical goddess of the moon. She scolds the witches for the 'trade and traffic with Macbeth/In riddles and affairs of death' (3.5.4–5) that they have undertaken without her. She, then, like the witches of the opening scene, makes a rendezvous with them. This time the meeting is not 'on the heath' but 'at the pit of Acheron', another reference to the classical mythology of the underworld. The song *'Come away, come away'* comes from off-stage and is the signal for her to depart.

Hecate appears again just after the witches have prepared the cauldron spell. This time it is with *'the other three witches'* (4.1.38). She approves of their action and suggests that they all

> now about the cauldron sing
> Like elves and fairies in a ring,
> Enchanting all that you put in.

(4.1.41–3)

The witches then dance to another song.

Most editors then provide an exit for Hecate and the mysterious 'other three witches' who do not appear elsewhere in the play. The 'second witch', presumably the same 'second witch' who has been in the earlier scenes, then reverts to the more familiar witching style with

> By the pricking of my thumbs,
> Something wicked this way comes.

(4.1.44–5)

and the scene continues with Macbeth's entrance. The Folio text, on the other hand, provides no exit for Hecate and the other three witches and it is at least possible for them to remain on stage to take part in the final dance, after the show of kings.

Editorial anxiety about this scene, signalled by the Middleton controversy and the changes to stage directions, occurs at least partly because of the strange mix of styles that occur in the Hecate scenes. The village witchcraft of maleficium that we have seen in the three witches' first scenes is repeated in the chanting round the cauldron but Hecate's classical origins and her invocation of set-piece songs seems to come from a quite different intellectual and theatrical tradition in which witches were a source of entertainment and an opportunity for learnedly informed display.[10] The thesis that Middleton added material (without rewriting the whole scene for a coherence of style) would explain that mix. It also addresses the fact that the cauldron scene, for all its significance in the play's narrative development, is a difficult scene to manage, as it stands, because of a tension between its narrative significance and the apparently extraneous witches' songs and dances.

After the display of kings and Macbeth's appalled reaction, the first witch[11] proposes some entertainment to offset the horror:

> But why/ Stands Macbeth thus amazedly?
> Come, sisters, cheer we up his sprites,
> And show the best of our delights.
> I'll charme the air to give a sound,
> While you perform your antic round:
> That this great king may kindly say,
> Our duties, did his welcome pay.
>
> *Music. The Witches dance, and vanish.*

(4.1.125–31)

This eclectic mix of horror and entertainment is somewhat at odds with interpretations that stress the play's psychic and ethical consistency. However, it does remind us that one of the writer's tasks – and one that he might have shared with others –

was to represent the witches on stage. This representation involved a set of theatrical choices about music and song as well as costume and use of the stage space.

The fairly simple technical demands of the witch scenes (discussed earlier, 9–11) drew on techniques that had been used in earlier plays. Marlowe's *Dr Faustus* had included a scene where the seven deadly sins parade across the stage to a commentary from Mephistophilis. The armed head, a convenient stage prop that no doubt reappeared as Macbeth's head in the play's finale, had also been seen before, rising from below the stage for supernatural effect in *Friar Bacon and Friar Bungay*, and *The Old Wives Tale.* These plays were from the old repertory inherited by the Admiral's Men, the rivals to Shakespeare's company. *Friar Bacon and Friar Bungay* had been performed by the Queen's Men in 1594 but was revived in 1603 with an additional prologue and epilogue by Thomas Middleton that made it suitable to take the play to court. Similarly, when William Bird and Samuel Rowley were paid for additions to *Dr Faustus* in 1602–3, it may also have been for a revival.[12]

The evidence of these revivals of old plays, that included magic processions and apparitions rising from below the stage, suggests that Shakespeare's development of the witch-scenes in *Macbeth* may have been part of the Chamberlain's/King's Men response to the 'several plays about magicians in performance in 1602–3'[13] produced by the rival company.

When *Macbeth* is set in the context of Admiral's Men revivals, we can see how its witches are connected to a traditional theatrical presentation of magic. By the turn of the century, this style of stage magic may have come to seem somewhat old-fashioned. The new boy's companies, playing in hall theatres whose seat prices were six times those of theatres like the Globe, were representing witches rather differently. Marston's *Sophonisba* presented a witch who was sinister in a sexualized way and whose role in the play was to acquire sex and provide sexual pleasure in disguise for the play's lascivious villain. This was also the direction taken by Middleton's *The Witch* in which the additional songs for *Macbeth* first appeared.

Where Shakespeare's witches take the initiative in tempting Macbeth, Middleton's are actively solicited by the characters who use their charms to fulfil their, mainly sexual, plotting.

Middleton's witches have much longer scenes in which they show off their witch-lore (as Shakespeare's witches do in 4.1.) and the details of their action refer much more directly to material taken from contemporary writings on witchcraft. In Middleton's play, the witches handle an 'unbaptised brat' on stage, a grotesque inflation of Shakespeare's 'finger of birth-strangled babe'; Middleton's witches are planning to boil the baby to make a flying ointment, using a recipe taken directly from a learned account of witches' magic powers.[14] Middleton's witches are much more explicitly bent on sexual satisfaction, including the casually shocking suggestion of incest between Hecate and her son.[15] Sexual desire informs all Middleton's witches' behaviour and is also the characters' main purpose in seeking their help. The sexual, rather than the supernatural, informs all their actions and the surrounding enchantment used to fulfil sexual desire is extrapolated from serious demonology and scientific writing in ways that might have both disgusted and excited an urban audience whose direct experience of village witchcraft was limited.

The songs that were suggested by first lines in the Folio of *Macbeth* fit Middleton's play much better and show the direction that witch material was taking in the King's Men's repertory. In the opening scene of *Macbeth*, the witches respond to the calls of village familiars, Paddock and Graymalkin, a frog and a cat. In Middleton's play, the song 'Come away, come away' is introduced as '*a spirit like a cat descends*' and the witches sing:

> A kiss, a coll, a sip of blood,
> And why stay'st thou so long
> I muse, I muse,
> Since the air's so sweet and good.

> (3.3.51–4)

These lines make clear the physical relationship between witches and their familiars that is never made explicit in *Macbeth*.

The differences between the magic in Middleton's *Witch* and Shakespeare's play suggest that the magic narratives of the revived older drama was being replaced by a different style of witchy theatricality that exploited the potential of the stage rather than drawing on deep beliefs about the witches' supernatural power. There were other signs that witches on stage may not have been solely the object of terror and awe. A satiric pamphlet from 1614, mocks a woman's extravagant spending on hair-pieces, claiming that her 'deformed perriwigs, . . . were fitter to furnish a Theatre, or for her that in a stageplay, should represent some hagge of hell'.[16] In the 1630s, the stage treatment of the horrific case of the Witches of Lancashire,[17] seems to refer back to *Macbeth* when a character mocks her mother's clothes as looking 'like one o'the Scottish wayward sisters'.

These observations give some indication that *Macbeth*, or a play that also involved Scottish witches, remained in the repertory. They also suggest a much more knowing approach to the theatre in which plays were a source of witty critical commentary that placed them in an entertainment world that was conscious of its own productions and expected the audience to be so too.

THE ADAPTED WORK

The tinkering additions that Middleton may have made to *Macbeth* might have kept the play up to date: they were certainly part of the process that all the theatre companies used to make the most of their back-list to extend their repertory. Through the seventeenth century, revivals and printing played an important role in making a play (a one-off event) into a work (a commodity that could be used again and again to keep the theatre business solvent). Throughout the seventeenth century, the London theatre scene displayed the mix of new work and revivals that has characterized every dynamic theatre repertory since. The revival of *Macbeth* in 1611 in the production seen by Simon Forman, the evidence for its adaptation by Middleton and the reference to it in a witch play from the 1630s all suggest that this play took its place in the shifting repertory that changed the play to suit new audience tastes.

The role of *Macbeth* in this repertory was critical for its survival into the period after the civil war had closed the London theatres for over twenty years. The two theatre companies that were established after the return of King Charles in 1660 had only a back-list to create their new repertory. That back-list of extant plays, including those of Shakespeare, was divided between them. In the shift around of play ownership, Shakespeare's plays were assigned to the Duke's company led by William Davenant, a playwright and theatre entrepreneur from before the civil war. Davenant undertook a major adaptation of the play and his version was used on the stage for the ensuing hundred years.

Davenant's wholesale adaptation of *Macbeth* began a significant shift in the idea of the writer and his work. He seemed keen to capitalize on Shakespeare's reputation in personal as well as literary terms. John Aubrey who wrote *Brief Lives* of a number of early-modern writers noted Davenant's claim that 'he writt with the very spirit that (did) Shakespeare and was contented enough to be thought his son'. Davenant's slur on his mother's chastity was reinforced by Aubrey's memory of her as a 'very beautiful woman, & of a very good witt and of conversation extremely agreeable'. More recent research has suggested that the connection between Shakespeare and the Davenant family had more to do with their shared connections to the Midland counties and to the profession of glove-making, the trade of both Shakespeare's father and Davenant's uncles. Shakespeare and the Davenant family seem to have moved in the same London circles and the story that Shakespeare was Davenant's godfather is perfectly believable if undocumented.[18] This mythologized personal relationship with Shakespeare the writer, extended the sense that Davenant was bringing his works to a new generation but it did not preclude Davenant rewriting the play to bring it up to date and to make it more suited to the new taste for elegant symmetry and a focus on personal relationships, motivated by moral dilemmas.

Davenant cleaned up the play by removing the puzzling topical comedy of the Porter's scene and the ugly on-stage violence of Banquo's murder and the killing of Macduff's family. He also paid close attention to the language. Shakespeare's complex elaborations of image and idea were smoothed out so that difficulty and ambiguity were removed. For example, when Macbeth returns to the stage after having been called to look on Duncan's murdered body, the 1623 Folio text gives him the following lines:

Had I but died an hour before this chance,
I had lived a blessed time, for from this instant,
There's nothing serious in mortality.
All is but toys: renown and grace is dead,
The wine of life is drawn, and the mere lees
Is left this vault to brag of.

(2.3.84–9)

This speech has to do the dramatic work of presenting Macbeth's faked surprise and horror to the company on-stage and also to suggest what has been lost in Duncan's death. The language moves from the abstraction of 'There's nothing serious in mortality' to the vivid but puzzling comparison between the end of life and draining the dregs (lees) of wine from a bottle. Davenant clarifies the image and the sentiment by simple adaptation. 'There's nothing serious in mortality' becomes 'There's nothing in it worth a good man's care' and the arresting and original image of 'wine of life' is simply left out. To a modern ear, familiar with the Shakesperean lines, Davenant's version seems flat footed but the power of Shakespeare's images comes from their ambiguity, the sense that they gesture towards a meaning just out of sight.

Davenant's approach to reworking the overall narrative similarly closed off ambiguity and made the play's moral and psychic world simpler. He extended the roles of Macduff and his wife so that those two characters presented a clearer moral alternative to Macbeth and his lady. Lady Macduff, in particular, is explicitly feminized as a devoted wife whose 'divided soul' follows her husband to the war (see 1.5.5–14).[19] She is a pacifist (1.5.22–8) careless of the temptations of greatness (3.2.17–21) and alert to the moral dangers of usurpation even when it is disguised as patriotism (3.2.). Above all, Lady Macduff's speeches introduce the motivating power of ambition as an abstract force into the play's thematic structure.

In an added scene, Macduff contemplates the significance of Duncan's death and Lady Macduff draws an abstract moral conclusion:

Ambition urg'd him to that bloody deed:
May you be never by ambition led:
Forbid it, heav'n, that in revenge you should
Follow a copy that is writ in blood.

(3.2.4–7)

This emphasis on an abstracted motif of male ambition is also made explicit in Macbeth's speeches. As Macbeth contemplates the arrival of his enemies he contrasts his masculine ambition with his love for his wife:

> The spur of my ambition prompts me to go
> And make my kingdom safe, but love which softens
> Me to pity her in her distress,
> Curbs my resolves.

> (4.4.10–13)

Lady Macbeth, now pursued by the ghost of Duncan, is filled with remorse and blames Macbeth's failure to control her:

> You were a man.
> And by the charter of your sex you should
> Have govern'd me, there was more crime in you
> When you obeyed my counsels, than I contracted
> By my giving it. Resign your kingdom now,
> And with your crown put off your guilt.

> (4.4.54–9)

Macbeth's concern for his wife humanizes his character but after her death he is free to pursue his destiny. The thematic contrast between love and ambition is summed up in the play's finale as Macbeth dies crying 'Farewell vain world/ And what's more vain in it, Ambition' (5.6.94). The complexity of Macbeth's changing view of the witches' and his own equivocation, his agonized and self-aware contemplation of evil are replaced with a single abstract motivation.

In Davenant's revised version, the witches play an important role in this change of emphasis from psychic complexity to ethically abstract motivation. The witches act to differentiate the moral position of the two men. They appear to Macduff and his wife, just at the point when Macduff is considering the terrible implications of Duncan's death. In this scene, their songs draw generalized conclusions about good and evil rather than relishing their own mischief:

> Ill deeds are seldom slow nor single
> Following crimes on former wait
> The worst of creatures fastest propagate
> Many more murders must this one ensue,
> As if in death were propagation too.

> (2.5.32–6)

107

Lady Macduff's reaction to the witches presents her fearless courage but it also associates disbelief in the power of witchcraft with the character's moral integrity. She reminds Macduff that 'None can fear ill, but those that merit it'; she is given a version of Banquo's lines – 'The messengers of darkness never spake/To men but to deceive them' (2.5.85–6); and she concludes 'Their words are like/Their shape; nothing but fiction' (2.5.93–4). Macduff's response underlines the moral authority of his wife's scepticism:

> Am I made bold by her? How strong a guard
> Is innocence? If anyone would be
> Reputed valiant, let him learn of you;
> Virtue both courage is, and safety too.

(2.5.73–6)

This connection between belief in witches and moral dereliction is extended to the relationship between Macbeth and his lady. When Lady Macbeth begins to fear the disastrous outcome of her husband's murderous action, she suggests that he resigns the crown. Having blamed his wife for fuelling the flame of his ambition, Macbeth now concludes, 'I must have better counsellors'. He makes an explicit choice between his wife's feminine morality and the witches' seduction to ambition. She, in turn, rejects the witches as a deformation of her womanhood and turns away from Macbeth's ambition:

> Curse on your messengers of hell. Their breath
> Infected first my breast. See me no more.
> As King your crown sits heavy on your head,
> But heavier on my heart: I have had too much
> Of kings already.

(4.4.63–7)

Davenant draws out and makes explicit a connection between witches, gender and morality. In his version of the play, women are naturally moral, sceptical of evil and lacking in ambition. Witches are associated with a deformed femininity which seduces men to ambition, successfully in the case of Macbeth, whose wife is morally suspect because insufficiently feminine, and unsuccessfully in the case of Macduff who is armed with his wife's innocent courage in the face of evil.

These changes in Davenant's version of the play have been connected to changes in the politics both of gender relations and witch-belief. In the public culture of the Restoration theatre, Davenant's play aligned itself with a royalist history of the previous quarter of a century. As Rebecca Rogers puts it, 'The adaptation martyrises Charles I, legitimates Charles II and stresses the criminally destablising effects of revolution'.[20]

This view of recent history presented the English civil war as a time of political usurpation fuelled by enthusiasm in religion and a resulting disruption of all hierarchies, including patriarchal hierarchies of gender. Richard Kroll has also suggested that the play may have had a particular topical resonance in its connection to the exhumation and desecration of the bodies of Oliver Cromwell and his political associates.[21] In that political culture, witches could be represented as forces of disorder, and a belief in witches as emblematic of the superstition of an earlier age. Davenant's reworking of Shakespeare's play imposed on it a political morality that was enacted in the relationships between men and women, articulated in terms of moral abstractions and dramatized in the theatrical opposition between humans and the supernatural. In doing so, he laid out a thematic structure for the play which made it available for modern critical approaches based on moralized characters and generalized political themes. By making the play's ethical oppositions explicit and by connecting those oppositions to abstractions such as 'ambition' or 'evil' Davenant created a work that would provide a space for the literary criticism that helped to ensure its survival into the modern world.

7

A Lasting Work

Davenant's 1674 version of *Macbeth* presented the work as a consistent narrative where characters, who spoke literal and grammatical sense, articulated their motives for action in terms of clear ethical oppositions. Although Davenant's version of the work is no longer admired, it laid down the deep structure for understanding the play as working through abstractions such as 'ambition' or 'evil', the commonplaces of nineteenth and twentieth century literary criticism. By bringing Shakespeare's play up to date, Davenant also widened the gap between the work, that remained fixed in the 1623 Folio text, and the play, that could respond to the changing technologies of theatre and the changing expectations of its audiences.

The 1674 text of Davenant's version describes the presentation of the play with 'all the Alterations, Amendments, Additions and New Songs: As it is now Acted at the Duke's Theatre'. It prints the full texts of the songs given as first lines in the Folio text and adds songs and dances. This version of the play dominated the stage for half a century and met the desire for a theatre that provided spectacle and variety as well as clearly defined moral sentiments. Samuel Pepys saw it three times. In December 1666 he admired it as 'a most excellent play for variety'; in January 1667 he found it 'a most excellent play in all respects, but especially in divertissement, though it be a deep tragedy' and on the 19 April he commented on the 'variety of dancing and music'.[1] For Restoration audiences there was no contradiction between theatricality and serious art and in the new century John Downes reported in his *Roscius Anglicanus* that

> The Tragedy of Macbeth, alter'd by Sir William D'Avenant; being drest in all its Finery, as new Cloath's, new Scenes, Machines (as flyings for the Witches), with all the Singing and Dancing in it, the

first Compos'd by Mr. Locke, the other by Mr. Channell and Mr. Joseph Priest. It being all Excellently perform'd, being in the nature of an Opera, it Recompenc'd double the Expence; it proves still a lasting Play.[2]

A 'lasting play' for Downes was simply one that continued to please theatre audiences. Modern genre distinctions between theatre and opera, or critical values that oppose the physical work of theatrical effects to the inherent meaning of a historical play, were less significant in Restoration theatre circles and 'Shakespeare' treated with rather less reverence. In the same year that Davenant's text was printed, the play was parodied in the epilogue to Thomas Duffet's *Empress of Morocco*. The Epilogue was 'spoken by *Heccate* and three Witches, according to the famous Mode of Macbeth'. Duffet mocked the theatrical effects of Davenent's production at the Duke's theatre with a display of thunder and lightning as 'Three witches fly over the Pit – Riding upon Beesomes and *Heccate* descends over the stage in a Glorious Charriot, . . . made of a large Wicker Basket.'

Duffet's witches are prostitutes, giving salaciously detailed accounts of sexual encounters with representatives of gentlemen in the audience to Hecate, their madame. The familiar metre of the witches' speeches and the recognizable poetic tags could be transformed into obscene ridicule:

> I pick'd Shop-keeper up, and went to th'Sun,
> He Houncht – and Houncht – and Houncht;
> And when h'had done,
> Pay me quoth I,
> Be damn'd you Whore: did fierce Mechanick cry;
> And most unlike a true bred Gentleman,
> Drunk as a Bitch he left me there in Pawn.
>
> (16–22)[3]

Duffet's travesty was as much an attack on a rival theatre as a considered response to Shakespeare's play. The theatre venue for the King's Company, rival to Davenent's Duke's, had burned down and Duffett contributed a number of satires that undermined their work. In performance, the play had become a cultural resource that could be taken apart and reused according to theatrical and topical needs. The story, known from sources other than Shakespeare's play[4] was used for social and political

111

satire, while the theatres who were not licensed to play serious drama, made use of the play's familiarity to produce the splendid spectacle of *The History, Murders, Life and Death of Macbeth* (at the Royal Circus theatre in 1809) or the 'Grand and Terrific Historical Caledonian Drama' with 'National Marches, Choruses, Contests and Processions' in *The Fatal Prophecy! Or The Scottish Regicide*.[5] *Macbeth* continued to prove a lasting play throughout the eighteenth century and various actors and theatrical entrepreneurs had no compunction about elaborating the physical effects, including extending the witch sequences with choruses of singing and dancing witches.[6]

Alongside this theatrical inventiveness that adapted and reworked the play, *Macbeth* was proving to be a valuable cultural resource for another developing cultural industry. The publishing house of Jacob Tonson and Sons, anxious to realize the value of their investment in the texts of Shakespeare's plays, commissioned a series of editions of the works of Shakespeare whose commentary and prefatory material expanded Shakespeare's reputation as a maker of lasting plays into a complex critical sense of his ability to transcend the time in which he wrote and to speak of ethical and aesthetic values to contemporary audiences. The work of their editors created new texts of the play in their frequent emendations of the original Folio[7] but it also generated controversy among competing authors about the extent to which those emendations reflected the true meaning and the nature of Shakespeare's genius. These controversies were eagerly taken up in the literary magazines and critical circles of the time, and the work continued to be reshaped into a source for critical debate and disquisition about the meaning of the play.

The dominant critical values focused on the moral power of Shakespeare's art, values which found an echo in Macbeth's speeches on conscience and morality. The narrative of evil overthrown was generalized by successive writers into moral statements about the workings of morality in the world. As the essayist Richard Steele put it:

> the least Deviation from the Rules of Honour introduces a Train of numberless Evils, and involves him in inexplicable Mazes. He that has entered into Guilt has bid Adieu to Rest, and every Criminal has

his Share of the Misery expressed so emphatically in the Tragedian: *Mackbeth shall sleep no more!*[8]

Steele's account of the play indicates how Macbeth's own moral capacity, his ability to understand his ethical position, had become a part of the play's aesthetic power. The line about Macbeth's sleeplessness was taken as a definition of a guilty conscience that might afflict 'every criminal' rather than being part of Macbeth's particular obsessive response to the scene of Duncan's murder.[9] The play about a king and the witches' prophecy is replaced by a description of a moral journey extrapolated from the narrative of Shakespeare's play:

> When his desires are sated, conscience, formerly active, but disregarded, overwhelms him with deep contrition. The state of his mind continues, till the regular appetites recover strength, solicit indulgence, and are obeyed ... And his life is thus divided between the extravagance of the illicit desire, and the despondency of repentance.[10]

Richardson's eloquent account of Macbeth's state of mind does not map onto the events as they unfold in the Folio text: if anything Macbeth is more contrite in his speeches before the murder. However, the point of this form of commentary was to display the ethical virtuosity of the critics and to turn *Macbeth* among other plays of Shakespeare into a place where that ethical virtuosity could be exercised.

The play was particularly well-suited to this moralizing attention since it contained the infinitely fascinating figure of Macbeth's lady. William Richardson took the view that she was 'too savage to be a genuine representation of nature',[11] a view that begged a number of questions about the lady's role in the play but allowed for general and continuing controversy, about the nature of the character, her true motivation and her relationship to the common view of women, that continues to this day.

The 'lasting play' that provided the theatre with a resource for adaptation and the edited work that offered a place on which to exercise imaginative criticism came together in the extraordinary achievement of David Garrick. As a contemporary of Samuel Johnson from Lichfield in the English Midlands, Garrick had access to the literary traditions of Shakespeare as well as having an acute sense of how to manage a theatrical career in the highly competitive London theatre of the mid-eighteenth century. His performances of the part of Macbeth, as with others of Shakespeare's heroes, were celebrated in painting, were often controversial, were widely discussed and even turned into a kind of notation to analyse his idiosyncratic way of speaking the verse. This cult of celebrity was very carefully managed by Garrick and his reputation secured by the way he surrounded his performances with commentary. He preceded his performance as Macbeth by publishing 'An essay on acting' that contrasted his aim for his performance with the ranting style of James Quin who had played the part at a rival theatre.[12] Garrick's admiring biographer, Arthur Murphy, claimed that Quin reacted to the news that Garrick was to present *Macbeth* as written by Shakespeare, by exclaiming 'What does he mean? Don't I play *Macbeth* as written by Shakespeare?'.[13] The writer and his work had ceased to be a single, recognizable, historical artefact and had become the site of contesting interpretation. Murphy's story was part of the carefully constructed myth of Garrick, still prevalent in theatre history, that makes him the creator of the modern, textually faithful, tradition of performing Shakespeare. In fact, Garrick retained some of the Davenant text and continued the practice of omitting the on-stage murder of Lady Macduff.[14] His achievement was to sustain interest in the play and the work by generating controversy about interpretation and connecting that controversy to the genius of 'Shakespeare' (and, incidentally, of Garrick himself).

In restoring more of Shakespeare's lines to the play, Garrick took advantage of the new editorial controversies to deepen the sense of complexity that he brought to the performance of the character. Textual editors could change emphasis by shifting punctuation or emending lines but Garrick's performances made these changes audible on the stage. His acting was presented as a new kind of work on the play that justified editorial tinkering in terms of the emotional truth that an actor could give it.

Arthur Murphy, Garrick's biographer and publicist, for example, took personal credit for Garrick's reading of the line about the effect of Duncan's blood on 'great Neptune's ocean' (2.2.58). He recorded that Garrick 'was for some time in the habit of saying, the *green-one red;* but upon consideration, he adopted the alteration, (Green, one-red) which was first proposed by this writer in the Gray's Inn Journal'.[15]

Murphy provided an elaborate justification for his reading and had it endorsed by Dr Johnson. However, like so many proposed changes to the text of Macbeth, it provided a solution to a non-existent problem. The Folio text reads, quite clearly, 'Making the Greene one, Red'. As it stands, the line is possibly a bit weak and it begs the question of which of the 'multitudinous seas' is the green one. There is no bibliographical evidence for making the change but Garrick's pause after 'Green' established the new reading as one that pleased the ear, gave further emphasis to the monosyllables of the final line and gave an air of spontaneity and originality to a completely commonplace thought.[16]

Garrick was also keen to use his actorly devices of pauses in mid-line to work his way through some of the more syntactically complex passages in the play. In Macbeth's soliloquy in 1.7, he imagines that Duncan's 'Virtues/ Will pleade like Angels, trumpet-tongued against/The deep damnation of his taking off'. Garrick introduced a long pause after 'Angels', making it clear that the comparison was between virtues and angels before expanding the metaphor to the image of their being 'trumpet tongued'. Some critics objected that the effect was to transfer the epithet from 'angels' to 'virtues' but Garrick defended his reading: 'The epithet may agree with either, but I think it more elegant to give it to the virtues, and the sense is the same'.[17]

Garrick's defence makes it clear that he was less concerned with pedantic questions about the transmission of the text than with elegant theatrical effect. Nevertheless, the effect of Garrick's defence and his engagement with critical readings of particular passages served to increase the sense of Shakespeare's 'difficulty', the idea that reading and performing Shakespeare requires particular literary and historical skills. He was thus able to use the growing sense of Shakespeare's genius as the energizing force for his vision of theatre as a place of ethical experience.

In a defiant prologue celebrating the continued functioning of his theatre after important actors had absconded to his rivals, he insisted

115

> Sacred to Shakespeare was this spot design'd
> To pierce the heart, and humanize the mind,

The prologue continued with a wry acceptance of the equal demands of commercial viability and the simpler task of meeting audience taste for theatrical divertissement. Nevertheless, here, as in his other extensive writing on the stage, Garrick insisted on the synergy between ethical, emotional and physical effects in the pleasures of his art. He claimed that 'Acting is an Entertainment of the Stage, which by calling in the Aid and Assistance of Articulation, Corporeal Motion, and Occular expression, imitates, assumes or puts on the various mental and bodily Emotions arising from the various Humours, Virtues and Vices incident to human nature'. Garrick was writing at a time when the relationship between the senses, the emotions and the ethical capacity of human beings was being intensely debated by scientists and philosophers as well as literary intellectuals. In applying their ideas to acting, he gave the profession a standing that elevated it above mere pleasure and he also forged a link between the emotional pleasure of theatre and physical action on the stage.

This new style of acting was presented by Garrick's admirers as identifying the unfolding manifestation of a fully ethically and psychically aware character. Describing his performance of the 'dagger scene', his biographer Arthur Murphy described how

> Garrick's attitude, his consternation, and his pause, while his soul appeared in his countenance, and the accents that followed astonished the spectators. The sequel was a climax of terror, till at last he finds it to be the effect of a disordered imagination and his conscience forces him to say, 'It is the bloody business, which informs/Thus to my eyes'.[18]

Murphy's sense that Garrick's acting made 'his soul appear in his countenance' was of a piece with his overall reading of the play. He summarized the play's ethical significance as

> the greatest moral lesson that ever was presented on the stage. It displays the power of conscience in the strongest light; it shews the fatality that attends wild ambition, and the folly of believing the false predictions of vile imposters, who pretend to have preternatural communications.[19]

There was a growing synergy, in other words, between the critical sense of the play's moral significance and Garrick's ability to present that on stage with an intensity that supported the pre-existing critical reading. In his own writing, Garrick tightened the connection between his style of physical performance and the manifestation of Shakespeare's genius and that connection was reiterated in commentaries (then and since) on Garrick's contribution to the stage and to Shakespeare's history and reputation. The epitaph on Garrick's tomb reads

> Though sunk in death the forms the poet drew,
> The actor's genius bade them breathe anew.[20]

In fact the words that Shakespeare wrote were anything but 'sunk in death'. There was intense commercial competition to reproduce them in editions both from the monopoly publishers and from the pirate publishers who wanted a share of the backlist of earlier literature to launch their own publishing companies.[21] Moreover the transfer of Shakespeare's genius to Garrick's genius was a move that, in both cases, hid the real work of commercial rivalry and the difficulties of theatrical management required to keep the plays on the stage.

Garrick's genius lay, according to his admirers, in transmitting the essence of the play to an audience that would share the emotional pleasures of its contemplation. That ethical essence was articulated by many contemporary critics as a capacity to share a common understanding of the nature of good and evil. Their accounts of the play's moral and aesthetic force were urged on readers and audiences and came to stand in for, and in some sense to disallow, alternative responses to the play. Reciting 'A Prologue on Shakespeare and his Writings', Garrick demanded 'And who (so hardn'd) can refuse to weep / When *Duncan* falls and *Glamis* murders Sleep!'[22]

In practice of course many audiences then and since have not necessarily been moved by the experience of the play. Even some viewers of Garrick's attempts to convey sensibility through gesture found his performances fussy and overblown: 'convulsive twitchings...a set of mechanical motions in constant use, the caricatures of gestures suggested by pert vivacity'.[23] His achievement in the theatre was to create a commercially successful theatre business based on innovative styles of

117

performance and to surround them with a literary discourse of genius that made an emotional response to Shakespeare a mark of a refined sensibility, capable of appreciating high art.

Both Garrick's own commentary on his artistic practice, and accounts of it given by his admirers, present an interesting paradox in the development of ideas about the role of theatre in communicating emotional truth. On the one hand, their insistence on the significance of written drama and the restoration of historical masterpieces was set against the purely physical theatre of Harlequin and the 'vaulting Turk'; on the other, they recounted stories that suggested that attention to the language of the original work was the least important part of the performer's art.

Murphy's biography of Garrick included two anecdotes of his impact on people who could not hear or understand the language in which he expressed himself but nonetheless were moved by the performance and grasped its inner meaning. During his travels in Europe, Garrick apparently gave an impromptu performance of the dagger scene from *Macbeth* before the Duke of Parma who spoke no English. According to Murphy,

> His words were not understood, but his countenance expressed every sentiment, and every turn of the passions...The Duke of Parma, and his party, acknowledged that this specimen gave them an idea of Shakespeare's superior genius, and the great excellence of an English actor.[24]

In an even more curious episode, Garrick received a poem from a deaf-mute who insisted that he understood all passions from Garrick's acting even though he could not hear the words:

> What need of sound? When plainly I descry
> Th'expressive features, and the speaking eye;
> That eye, whose bright and penetrating ray
> Does Shakespeare's meaning to my soul convey.
> Blest commentator on great Shakespeare's text!
> When Garrick acts, no passage seems perplext.[25]

In the subsequent discussion, the deaf man explained that Garrick's power of communication was perfect because 'his face was a language'. This use of language as a metaphor for, rather than as an instrument of, communication drew on the

118

contemporary science of physiognomy: the idea that facial expressions provided a route into understanding the character and even the ethical tendencies of individuals.[26] Its implication for the reception of Shakespeare's play was very significant indeed. The essence of the play revealed in performance consisted not of language or narrative but an emotional experience, directly communicated from performer to spectator. It liberated the performers from the demands of the text and allowed interpretation to float free. Performers could make the play their own, while simultaneously adding their version as a new truth within the infinite possibility of the play's meaning. In 1794, for example, the actor Philip Kemble chose to ignore the stage instruction 'Enter ghost' throughout the banquet scene. His Macbeth ranted and recoiled from an empty space, allowing the theatre audience to share the courtiers' astonishment that he 'looked but on a stool'. Kemble was able to make this change since he could assume that his audience would know the play well enough to remember that a ghost appears at this stage. The effect, often repeated in subsequent performances, is to place the audience outside Macbeth, denying them a shared experience of the horror of the gory locks and the twenty trenched gashes on the figure who appears on stage. It also emphasizes the sense that the real concern of the play is with Macbeth's interior struggle rather than the events to which he responds.

The communication of characters' interiority was particularly significant in the construction of the role of Macbeth's lady. Writing of Mrs Siddons' famous rendition of the part, William Hazlitt wrote that

> it was in bursts of indignation, or grief, in sudden exclamations, in apostrophes and inarticulate sounds that she raised the soul of passion to its height, or sunk it in despair.[27]

Lady Macbeth's character, in other words, consisted not only in her famous speeches. They were merely clues that led into a deeper understanding of character that could be communicated by means uncircumscribed by textuality or traditional stage business. A performer could suggest a life that transcended the lines on the page and indeed a character who appeared in less than half of the scenes could dominate interpretations of the play. This direct, extra-textual relationship between the audience and the actor fed back into critical accounts. Descriptions of performance became a standard feature of the commentary in the *New Variorum* editions of *Macbeth* where actors' articulations of some of Shakespeare's most complex lines were accepted as the ones most likely to give them meaning. Textual debates were transferred to the theatre as new readings were given lengthy justifications in terms of Elizabethan stage and poetic practice.

In the early twentieth century, some of these interpretations were codifed by A.C. Bradley in series of notes to the lectures that made up his influential book, *Shakespearean Tragedy*.[28] His long note asking 'Did Lady Macbeth really faint?' illustrates the point. He addresses Lady Macbeth's single-line call for help in the midst of the 'scene of confusion where Duncan's murder is discovered' and enquires 'Does Lady Macbeth really turn faint or does she pretend?' The revealing word in his questions is 'really'. In one sense there is no 'really': we are witnessing a play, not a narrative of events which did occur at some other time; the text provides no evidence one way or the other; nothing in the narrative or progression of the action hangs on it. The process of Bradley's argument is as interesting as the question he begins with and has since provided a paradigm for interpretative criticism. He takes other episodes from the play – Lady Macbeth's return to the scene of the murder, her emotional collapse in Act 3 and suicide in Act 4 – as illustrative of an essential personality. He also canvasses reasons why she might have pretended to faint – to deflect attention from her husband's false reaction to the news of the murder – and he provides additional stage business for an ideal performance suggesting that even though she has no additional lines, the interval between the first and second call to attend to the lady is 'occupied in desperate efforts on her part to prevent herself from giving way, as she sees for the first time something of the truth to which she was formerly so blind, and which will destroy her in the end.'[29]

His conclusion is particularly telling:

Shakespeare, of course, knew whether he meant the faint to be real: but I am not aware if an actor of the part could show the audience whether it was real or pretended. If he could, he would doubtless receive instructions from the author.[30]

120

Bradley tries to place the ultimate authority for the text's meaning in the intentions of its author. However he also recognizes that the text alone provides no clue to those intentions. As a result, the play's meaning must rest in interpretation of its unspoken truth, informed by assumptions about human nature and assisted by accounts of performance. It assumes a consistency between character and action and locates personality in conventional assumptions about a gendered morality assumed to lie behind the text.

Bradley's account of Lady Macbeth echoes the *Variorum* editor's preoccupation with the faint as the key to her essential character. One of the many commentaries on that scene in the *Variorum* text articulates the expected ethical and emotional response to Lady Macbeth's dilemma:

> Call her a Fiend – she was a woman. Down stairs she comes – and stands among them all, at first like one alarmed only – astounded by what she hears – and striving to simulate the ignorance of the innocent – 'What in our house? Too cruel anywhere!' What she must have suffered then Shakespeare lets us conceive for ourselves.[31]

The commentary turns the play into a novel in which the work's combination of poetry and theatre is replaced by the characters' emotional journey that they share with their readers. The pleasure of the play rests in its capacity to engage the reader's or the audience's ethical imagination. The scope for controversy is endless, because it depends on that imagination rather than on the details of the Folio text.

The culmination of this imaginative recreation of the play and the source of its continuity into later criticism comes in Sigmund Freud's essay on 'Some character types met with in Psycho-analytic work'.[32] In that essay, Freud takes his observations about real-life psychoanalytic patterns and applies them seamlessly to literary characters as though their fictional behaviour can be interpreted in the same way. In a closely argued essay, he used Lady Macbeth and her husband as the paradigm that will encapsulate the behaviour of 'Those wrecked by success'. He describes 'the thesis that people fall ill of a neurosis as a result of *frustration* ... when a deeply rooted and long cherished wish has come to fulfillment'. He first describes Lady Macbeth as 'an example of a person who collapses on reaching success, after striving for it with single-minded energy'.[33] He speculates on

121

the conventional reading and then rejects the suggestion that Lady Macbeth's collapse in Act 4 is merely because her 'concentration and high tension' could not endure. He offers instead the more psychologically complex reading that Macbeth and his lady are driven by their unfulfilled desire for children. He further complicates this point with the suggestion that Shakespeare 'often splits a character up into two personages, which, taken separately, are not completely understandable and do not become so until they are brought together into a unity'.[34] Macbeth and his lady, he contends, cross over and exchange their personalities:

> What he feared in his pangs of conscience is fulfilled in her; she becomes all remorse and he all defiance. Together they exhaust the possibilities of reaction to the crime, like two disunited parts of a single psychic individuality.[35]

Freud's account of the play is a masterpiece of subtle close-reading. In a method established by the critical thinking of his time, it deals with the key episodes and speeches. However, it makes no reference at all to the issues of kingship and witches that inform the narrative. The words and actions of the play have been reconfigured into the work that presents a different story of psychic breakdown that builds on and replaces the ethical narrative of earlier criticism. Freud scrupulously acknowledges the then received wisdom on the play's historical origins as a '*pièce d'occasion* written for the accession of James' but connects that historical location with the concerns of Queen Elizabeth's childlessness. However, that historical existence is merely a drag on the play's more important significance as a way into understanding the psychic truth about human nature.

The appeal of a reading that reveals psychic or ethical truth is all the greater if it requires complex intellectual or imaginative work. Freud's essay provides this appeal both because of the subtlety of his extrapolation from the text and because he insists on the obscurity of the play's psychoanalytic meaning. He deepens the reading by connecting it to the paradox that Elizabeth's childlessness made James, the son of her murdered cousin, her heir. At the same time, he refuses to allow the historical reading to be definitive:

> We must, I think, give up any hope of penetrating the triple layer of obscurity into which the bad preservation of the text, the unknown intention of the dramatist and the hidden purport of the legend have become condensed.[36]

The historical play is abandoned behind 'the triple layer of obscurity' and the imaginative artefact floats free, carrying with it a potential for interpretation and recreation that will meet the needs of readers and audiences in succeeding centuries.

8

The Abstract Work

By the beginning of the twentieth century *Macbeth* had been re-formed by the work of critics and performers. In its high cultural version, it offered an account of two extraordinary people whose eloquent response to the deadly actions they had chosen provided a unique insight into the ethical and psychic workings of the human spirit. That insight could be traced back to particular speeches and episodes in the text of the play. The passages dealing with Macbeth's physical experience of fear and dread (see above 88), the physical effects of his regret in sleeplessness and paranoia and Lady Macbeth's sleep walking scene became paradigms for the ethical sensibility that was the mark of Shakespeare's genius. The continuing appeal of this ethical take on the work arose because it recreated and eloquently articulated eighteenth-century views about the nature of ethical sensibility. It was also a result of the way that the experience of the play had entered the cultural awareness of the population. As William St Clair has explained, the great folio collected editions of Shakespeare were too expensive to achieve a wide readership and pirate publishers had attempted to break into the market with collections and anthologies of poetry that they could claim were not covered by universal copyright.[1] The copyright publishers responded with their own anthologies of 'Beauties' that built on the practice in early editions of identifying with quotation-marks passages that the editor felt were particularly fine. The anthologies glossed the passages with abstractions – Love, fear, death etc – and often arranged them in illustrative groups. The knowledge of the play, especially for those who did not buy it in expensive folio editions or did not live within reach of notable productions, was thus transformed into memorable lines. Poetic abstraction became meaning, the play became a palimpset of significance whether it was being re-edited or reproduced in the theatre. *Macbeth*, like other early-modern plays and poetry, became known by its 'beauties'. The eloquent statement of common-places – such as Macbeth's hysterical disquisition on sleep in 2.4. – were removed from their dramatic contexts so that their poetic truths came to seem self-evident, not least because of their familiarity. The great speeches and key moments, given intense and subtle renditions on the stage, came to stand in for the historical artefact produced by the King's Men and the printers of the folio text in the early seventeenth century.

Critical admiration and dissemination of these new versions of the work was only one aspect of its reproduction. Once it was cut free from its history by Davenant's adaptation and the interventions of editors, it could also be re-produced in a variety of settings that extended its appeal to different audiences. This variety of reproduction, directed at different audiences and used for different purposes was to be expected. The market for culture expanded in line with the growth of the economy as a whole and a work whose copyright could be contested through adaptation, and whose narrative and setting invited elaboration was a valuable resource. Moreover, the growing entertainment and cultural business was accompanied by a growth in news-paper and magazine commentary in which cultural brokers, including some of the best known writers of the day, both recorded and judged these transformations as they occurred. Together they created the work as an object of criticism and commentary that established and constantly renewed the terms and significance of its reproduction. This activity added to the sum of intellectual pleasures which the play afforded and ensured its continuing status as a work of high culture. That status, however, depended as much on the interaction among critical views as it did on the particular features of the play itself.

The cultural work that surrounded Shakespeare and *Macbeth* was given a significant new impetus by the establishment of Shakespeare as a significant part of the curriculum of schools and universities in the early twentieth century. The new critical discourses that developed in educational establishments distin-guished themselves from the work in the theatre by restoring an awareness of the transmission of the original texts and theatrical conventions. They also needed to establish a distance from the ways of discussing Shakespeare that had been established by an earlier generation of critics and performers.

One of the most influential of these interventions was made by the Cambridge critic, Lionel Knights. In his famously sarcastic title, 'How Many Children had Lady Macbeth?', he repudiated the critical excrescences that seemed to him to have clouded appreciation of the essential nature of Shakespeare's work. He offered his essay as a critique of Bradley's concern with 'character issuing in action' which Knights blamed for

> all the irrelevant moral and realistic canons that have been applied to Shakespeare's plays, for the sentimentalising of his heroes ... and his heroines.[2]

He proposed instead to deal with 'Shakespeare primarily as a poet', arguing that the only way to deal with the particular power of the play was

> To allow full weight to each word, exploring its tentacular roots, and to determine how it controls and is controlled by the rhythmic movement of the passage in which it occurs.[3]

The resulting analysis has proved enormously influential, highlighting passages which it is now impossible for any critic to ignore: the passages dealing with confusion created by paradox (1.1.10–11; 1.2.7–9), the passage that identifies the ambiguous gender of the witches (1.3.43–4) and above all the passages which speak of a concern with the deformation of nature and traditional order in relations between men.

Knights' concern was to use the Shakespearean poetry as an eloquent statement of absolute truth and to instruct his readers not only about that truth but also in the acquisition of skills of reading which would fortify them against what he regarded as the numbing banality of commercialized mass culture in 'the era of the Daily Mail and the Best Seller'. Although he claimed to be investigating 'exactly why the lines are so and not otherwise', Knights had nothing to say about their textual transmission or their relationship to versions of those ideas in other early modern writing. Nor is there any formal analysis of the metrics or lexis of the chosen passages. The lines are so and not otherwise because they offer a coherent interpretative truth which is to be found in their sum rather than in their relationship to narrative or action. Where Bradley and Johnson had identified interpretation in the gaps between the text and its audience or within the narrative, Knights was able to gloss the gaps by offering a seamless connection from one heightened passage to another, illuminated by his own eloquent commentary on the significance of the poetry.

Knights does not comment on, and may not have been aware of, the fact that many of the passages he chose had already been identified in the anthologies of Shakespeare's 'beauties'. The power of his essay lies in the fact that he works across a terrain that earlier criticism had already mapped and made familiar. At no point does Knights identify reasons for his choice of passages. They all contribute to its overall meaning that was summed up in the opening assertion: 'Macbeth is a statement of evil'. The evil that Knights identifies is not merely the evil of regicide but a rupture in the 'system of values that gives emotional coherence to the play'. Those values of nature and order were conterminous with the values of the group of intellectuals who found, in English literature and poetry in particular, the possibility of a resistance to the deformations of industrialized modern culture.[4]

This process of creating meanings for the play involved more than the inventiveness of individual critics. It was linked to social and historical processes. As Francis Mulhern has shown, the Scrutiny group, of which L. C. Knights was an important member, was animated by its participants' sense of exclusion from the dominant commercial culture. They articulated the need for writers on literature and the arts to offer an ethical critique of cultural developments. The passion with which they did this was informed both by a sense of scant control which they could exercise in culture and by a concomitant commitment to the importance of literary education.

Knights read the play as a vision of the destruction of a naturally ordered community. The feeling and ethical thought processes of the characters were replaced by the vision of the critic, endorsed by his sophisticated reading of the verse. His commentary drew out connected meaning and images that replaced the details of the play's narrative and its criticism throughout its history. Knights' methodology that rearranged connecting images and speeches into an abstract pattern proved to be as influential as his conclusions about their meaning. This separation between the narrative and material theatricality of the play, together with an emphasis on its imagery and poetic movement laid it open to a contest over meaning which came as much from the needs of the critics as from the play itself.

This new version of the play that emphasized its poetic pattern also met the quite different needs of a new generation of critics. In the 1960s and 1970s cultural and political change impacted on the reception of the writer and his work. In the United Kingdom, new injections of state funding into education and the arts had brought with them demands for democratization and accountability. They extended the reach of culture and responded to the demands of a wider section of the population. The demands for 'relevance' in the arts and education, though stoutly resisted by those who regarded themselves as the guardians of high culture, produced readings and productions of Shakespeare's plays which tried to speak to a modern moment and in particular to negotiate in cultural form the ways in which the society was changing. Those who saw in the early modern world a mirror of their own troubled and changing time, challenged the valorization of an organic world view, a claim for a world at one with nature and tradition, which had animated the Scrutiny group. This generation of critics was more at ease with the products of mass culture but was fiercely critical of their society's failure to address the inequalities of gender and race. For many of them Shakespeare and his work were tainted by an implied association with high culture but for others the appropriation of Shakespeare's meaning became part of a new political agenda.

Knights' abstraction of the play as a disquisition on ethical rupture was assimilated into feminist and political readings in which those ruptures were identified explicitly with the conflict between men and women. One feminist critic, Janet Adelman, took the process of abstraction one stage further. Macbeth and his lady were seen not as representative men and women (their story was too exceptional for that). They were seen instead as representing 'images of a masculinity and a femininity that are terribly disturbed.'[5] The shift from individual figures in an old play to abstract embodiments of masculinity and femininity was effected partly by a sense that the work must speak of larger truths and partly by the psychoanalytically informed idea that art deals in archetypes that oppose the masculine principle of 'authority' and the feminine principle of 'nurturance'. The story of Macbeth is made universal, not because its narrative is repeated in modern times but because it represents the universal questions of the ways in which repeatedly fractured relationships might be resolved.

The details of Adelman's account of the play could be contested: not everyone would agree that Duncan is the image of 'the father as the androgynous parent from whom, singly, all good can be imagined to flow'.[6] Equally, some might object that Lady Macbeth does not actually murder her child in adopting a masculine role to encourage Macbeth, and the connection made between Lady Macbeth and the witches takes no account of their different approaches to the supernatural or the fact that they never meet. However, these details are less significant than the method by which particular events from the play are extrapolated from narrative and given a symbolic significance that lies above the events of the play. This critical process literalizes the play's metaphors so that the most controversial interpretation depends less on a shared sense of real human behaviour and more on the resonant echoes created in the language of the chosen passages. Thus the association of Duncan with the source of all growth comes from his lines to Banquo: 'I have begun to plant thee and will labour/ To make thee full of growing' (1.4.28–9). Macbeth's image of the poisoned chalice is rescued from its cliché'd modern meaning through an association with the banquet disrupted by Banquo's ghost which is then generalized into an image of nurturance associated with the archetypal feminine. When Lady Macbeth calls on the spirits that tend on mortal thoughts to take her milk for gall, Adelman literalizes the wish as fantasy and connects it to the charge that witches nursed the devil: 'Lady Macbeth and the withes fuse at this moment and they fuse through the image of perverse nursery.'[7]

The intellectual consistency of the reading draws the whole play into itself, complete with its historical and literary references. Macbeth's dagger speech, that imagines 'Murder' moving 'with Tarquin's ravishing strides', turns Duncan's murder into rape and when Macduff imagines Duncan's body as having the blinding effect of a Gorgon – 'Approach the chamber and destroy your sight/With a new Gorgon' (2.3.65–6) – the connection between Duncan and a rape victim is complete. Psychoanalytic theory read the myth of the Gorgon, who blinded any man who looked at her, as the image of a man appalled by the vision of the castrated female. Adelman invokes that dark memory to explain Macduff's image of the horror that Duncan's murdered body will produce. The power of these connected images lies in its suggestion that Duncan's bloodied body, with its multiple wounds, has been revealed as female and hence will blind his sons. There is no suggestion that this thought process was explicit in the mind of either the characters or their creator. The reading is held together by the framework of Freudian psychoanalysis which is itself informed by images and narratives taken from Freud's reading of Greek literature. Freud read these narratives as symbolic of the primary drives of the unconscious. Atavistic desires for violent and forbidden sexual fulfillment were suppressed by the conscious mind but could be enacted in fantasy, such as the Greek myths of parricide and incest. Shakespeare's language was also informed by references to classical narratives and the coincidence of these references allows a movement between the often baffling eclecticism of Shakespeare's imagery and the readings which Freud drew from classical literature.

The reader is thus engaged in an interpretative process which links a knowledge of psychoanalysis to the aesthetic impact of the text. The reader need no longer be engaged by a narrative of regicide which might seem a less resonant ethical problem in the twentieth century. There can instead be an appreciation of the text's potential for articulating deeper truths about the unconscious drives of sexuality and the misaligned power relations between women and men.

The all-encompassing nature of this reading allowed it to assimilate all the puzzling and inconsistent elements in the play. The witches which had been the focus of critical scepticism since Dr Johnson's critical interventions, were stripped of any historical specificity. They could be assimilated into the reading by being turned into the principles of the 'destructive power of female chaos'. This, in turn, is developed into a link between the witches and Lady Macbeth's infanticidal fantasy which elides her female destructiveness with the witches' power. The further link to the bloody children of the witches' apparitions, Macduff's murdered son and the infant Macduff, bloody from being 'from his mother's womb/Untimely ripped' (5.9.15–16), then seems irresistible. These murdered children, who might include the 'birth-strangled babe', are felt to destroy the promise of maternal nurture, enforce a bloodthirsty masculinity on Lady Macbeth and ensure the triumphant return of Macduff who is not 'of woman born'.

This pattern of symbolic connections, like Knights' analogous pattern, all but overwhelms the play's narrative of regicide and revenge. The story of witches and ghosts, a wicked queen and a murdered king is no longer satisfying to the sophisticated critic. Instead, the play's narrative movement is replaced by a coherent symbolic structure. The play's suspense about the fulfilment of prophecy, its final opposition between hero and villain or the dramatic ironies of Macbeth's misery in power seem trivial compared with the enactment of the universal psychic drama of conflict between male and female principles. That drama seems to provide a much more satisfactory account of the play's aesthetic power, its poetic richness and its continuing emotional appeal. Moreover the complexity of that reading depends on a sophisticated understanding both of Freud's castration theory of sexuality and the feminist critique of Melanie Klein, Hélène Cixous and the French feminists.[8] As such, it offers a more satisfying intellectual experience that, like Knights's essay, rescues the play from the easy identification with commonplace human experience and makes it instead the locus of deeper psychoanalytic truth.

In the twentieth century, *Macbeth* offered particularly resonant material for this method in the theatre as well as in critical writing. The story of the play is very well known, its narrative is very simple and it sets supernatural temptation and human misdemeanour side by side in ways that invite analogy with any number of similar situations. Once the play's key figures have been abstracted into archetypes, the witches, the king, the murderer and the wicked queen seem as open and as suggestive as tarot cards, able to be rearranged in different combinations for different purposes.

131

For twentieth-century theatre artists, often self-consciously seeking an alternative to the realist style of commercial theatre, *Macbeth* has provided an ideal opportunity to produce creative work based on abstracted images and motifs from the play. The witches in particular seemed to provide the inspiration for theatrical images that made the internal connections more resonant and connected the play to the audience's world. For Edward Gordon Craig, for example, they were the embodiment of Macbeth's and his lady's desire for power:

> We should see them...offering the woman a crown for her husband, flattering her beyond measure, whispering to her of her superior force, of her superior intellect; whispering to him of his bravery.[9]

For Komisarjevsky in 1923, they were scavengers looting the battlefield, in an image that had a particularly powerful impact in the aftermath of the First World War, and has been used on many occasions since. The play was made to speak not merely of a conflict among Scottish and Scandinavian warlords but of war and conflict in general. Overloaded with meaning, the witches could speak of the aboriginal gods angry at the destruction of their ancient landscape (Footsbarn 1993); they could represent the shaga in a re-enactment of the tribal wars of South Africa; or they could be feral children scurrying along the windswept balconies of a Birmingham housing estate.[10] Like the Balinese art forms or African masks or the improvised performances of *commedia dell' arte* that had inspired modernist theatre practice, the witches seemed to offer directors a route into a world beyond the rational and to offer the possibility of a theatre that would connect its audience to dark primeval forces. The significance of the work spilled beyond the boundaries of narrative and history and became a kind of creative resource for the theatre practitioner's imagination.

The development of the theatrical work came more and more to be set in defiant opposition to the literary work. Reviewing Orson Welles's 1936 production for the Negro Unit of the Federal Theatre project, Robert Little noted that the play appealed as much to white down-town New Yorkers as to the audience in Harlem:

> The whites went to see *Macbeth*, not to hear Shakespeare, who had bored most of them at school, but to get something different – that

> something at once more innocent and richly seasoned, child-like and jungle-spiced, which is the gift of the Negro to a more tired, complicated and self-conscious race.[11]

Little's racial stereotypes now seem crass and were contested at the time by African-American intellectuals. However, they are redolent of practitioners' desire for a theatre that would transcend the text and offer a more authentic experience that drew on but gave no authority to the historical writer and his work.

In this contest for ultimate authority over the work, its meanings are often reduced to banal commonplace and contrasted with the greater vitality of the theatre experience. Charles Marowitz, whose collages of Shakespeare's plays transformed their representation in the theatre in the mid-twentieth century, was particularly contemptuous of the 'footling' critical contest over 'the definitive meaning of the work'. Instead he celebrated the contemporary cultural moment in which variety, plurality and innovation were significant values:

> We've had a Christian Macbeth; a Gangster Macbeth; an Oriental Macbeth; a Primitive Macbeth; a Political Macbeth; why not a jinxed Macbeth?[12]

The eclectic plurality which Marowitz celebrated was made possible by the abstracting moves of modernist criticism but he has no need to acknowledge or even recognize that process. He is able instead to rehearse the drama of innovation in which his vision of the play is created in opposition to the views of a dominant critical establishment. As a theatre practitioner, however, he could impose his reading on the performance. He used the power of the theatre to make the audience share the distorted psychotic vision that he offers as Macbeth's.

Marowitz's aim was to liberate the play from being 'a sermon on the inescapability of retribution', the banal reiteration of what he sarcastically calls 'the highly original fact that crime doesn't pay'.[13] He achieved this liberation from commonplace moralizing by creating startling theatrical effects that presented the action as a set of extended psychotic fantasies. The murder of Lady Macduff and her child, for example, was enacted by the witches wearing the costumes of Macbeth's soldiers. Even the action of Macbeth's destruction was an echo of his obsession with the witches: Birnam wood was brought on stage in the form of witches' brooms. The play was released from the particularity of its narrative by a set of juxtapositions that connect the key images, turning critical extrapolation into theatrical effect.

The result of these innovations in staging was to change the conception of the play from a narrative enacted by characters whose action could be judged in ethical terms, to a patterned artistic experience, dominated by a central idea. That central idea could be created out of a sense of characters' motivation – the sub-text of nineteenth-century theatre practice – or it could be connected to larger ideas about the nature of the play's world – the theme of modernist Shakespeare criticism.

For Marowitz, and for many directors since, the dominating idea involved no more than a new reading of the characters' motivation, albeit expressed in contemporary terms. Marowitz described Macbeth as 'a man in the final stages of hallucinatory breakdown' and structured his collage/play in ways that allowed the audience to share some of Macbeth's hallucinations. It was an approach that made sense of the supernatural, the dagger, the witches, the obsession with murdered sleep and it echoed the values of a culture in which the language of psychology was contesting the language of morality. The theatrical representation of more complex ideas about the *world* of the play and the fundamental nature of its key relationships depended as much on the designer as the director. The play's setting and the key note set by the witches' opening scene were used to establish a sense of horror and of a world in a state of decay and alienation, while Macbeth and his lady acted out the destruction of their hopes of greatness.

These developments in criticism and theatre practice liberated the play to create new meanings and became the starting point for some of the twentieth century's most significant works of art worldwide. Abstract ideas about *Macbeth*'s world and a stripped down narrative of murder and its consequences have been transferred to other cultural traditions and presented in the classic film versions of Kurosawa and Ninagawa, Welles and Polanski.[14] These new works use Shakespeare as a source, much as Shakespeare himself used Holinshed or the suggestive visual motifs of *Newes from Scotland*.

Seen from the perspective of the twenty-first century, these shifts around Shakespeare in criticism and theatre appear as part of the logic of modernism. As Hugh Grady explains,

> Everything associated with ... 'historical values' – narrative, character, teleology, and time as an orderly linear narrative – became recoded as aesthetically passé; and painting and literature ... replaced history with myth, linear narrative with simultaneity, and linear time with forms more complex and multi-layered.[15]

That modernist tendency is still apparent in the eclecticism of forms on which the theatre can draw and the ways that the play is available world wide for multiple styles and interpretation.

What is more remarkable now is the way that 'Shakespeare' is also used as the locus of a debate about innovation and modernity. 'Shakespeare' is required both to represent the transcendent values of tradition and to be the space for new forms of creativity. The defiant and often reductive critique of 'traditional' or 'school' Shakespeare that characterized modernist critics and theatre practitioners is now placed firmly on one side of the discussion, while creative, free, theatrical Shakespeare is placed on the other. This debate continues in spite of over a century of modernist theatre practice, half a century of publicly funded experimental theatre and at least a quarter of a century of innovative work on the pedagogy of Shakespeare in education. The cultural pressures that continue to fuel this debate are connected to the role of Shakespeare in compulsory education and the constant struggle to ensure continued public funding for the arts. Its effect is to substitute the debate over 'Shakespeare' for the more difficult question of how we are to value and make use of the art of the past. The debate also preempts discussions of the absolute aesthetic quality of particular renditions of the play since statements about aesthetic value can be easily shifted into position-taking about the value of Shakespeare.

The sheer number of productions of the play worldwide, and the sheer range of different contexts in which it appears, from children's art work to the therapy of psychotic prisoners,[16] means that the free-play of *Macbeth* has long ago escaped the work printed in the Folio of 1623. The results have to be judged by the context of the work: they can be a banal or parasitic analogizing that uses the work's reputation and cachet to give significance to a clichéd retelling of the old story; or they can be a recreation of the material for stunning new effect.

Analysing this transformation of the work into new kinds of play is extremely challenging. The integrity of its artistic purpose (and in some cases its tangible social benefit) cannot be in doubt. The resulting work also often produces aesthetic effects that are powerful because of their mix of the familiar story and the strange and novel visual images or performance styles. The work as an object of contemplation or interpretation has been replaced by the moment-by-moment experience of play that cannot be translated back into any comprehensive or unitary interpretation.

Descriptions of this kind of work, though fascinating as reportage, cannot substitute for the experience so there can be no shared basis for judgement or critique. The work of the play is either tightly tied to an instrumental social purpose or is reproduced (often in the metropolis, far from the lives of those it was designed to affect) as a playful representation of work whose aesthetic is made up of exotic effects given an added resonance by the knowledge of its original moment of production.

This creative appropriation of *Macbeth* in the theatre and for social purposes is further complicated by efforts to adapt it directly into the styles and formats of mainstream entertainment. For example, the 2005 'Shakespeare Retold' series on BBC television took the play's narrative of insubordinate treachery and situated it in a restaurant kitchen where a commis chef is driven to murder the restaurant owner because he is resentful that his work in gaining the restaurant's reputation is overlooked. Once again, the narrative is abstracted into the key elements of murder and revenge and bloody violence that are performed with complete commitment by actors in the style of television naturalism. The witches, too, are naturalized into passing refuse collectors, alien only in that they come from a 'seagull-strewn landfill'.[17] Lady Macbeth, of course, makes her appearance as the ambitious wife, managing the front of house for the restaurant.

The reviews for this piece, on the whole, took it at face value, discussing it in the terms that would be used for any week-night

TV. Some acknowledged the reduction in size and scope – 'Shakespeare's tragedy is too big and bloody to fit comfortably into this modern setting'[18] – but every effort was made to admire the show as a welcome opportunity to see new drama on screen: 'the BBC needs to encourage original television dramatists and this is the way to do it'.[19]

The Writer and his Work, however, still cast a long shadow. The reviews often had a defiant tone, justifying their approval of the adaptation with reference to earlier practice but anxiously insisting that the end result would be a return to some authentic idea of 'Shakespeare':

> Why not reinterpret stories that Shakespeare used? It's been done loads of times over the centuries – they're good stories, and a good fresh take on one of them can reflect interestingly on the original.[20]

The BBC was nevertheless anxious about this apparent act of lese majesty. They hired distinguished academics to provide a learned commentary that could be accessed using interactive technology. The broadsheet newspapers, too, claimed that adaptations would bring teenagers back to read the original texts. Both the adaptation and the response revealed the new role of *Macbeth* and Shakespeare in providing a location where twenty-first century cultural values could be repeatedly re-hearsed but always left unresolved.

The production of a new work for television was felt to require an independent aesthetic evaluation but its evident base in Shakespeare muddied the terms in which that evaluation could be expressed. One review segued from a discussion of a reality TV show 'Big Brother' to *Macbeth*, noting that 'The script doffed its cap to the Bard, but was not afraid to show us a new, dark, claustrophobic 21 century piece of work'.[21] The shift from reality TV, that certainly provides high levels of unmediated emotion, to a narrative drama with a more structured, if less immediate, management of audience response reproduced the experience of contemporary television. The fortuitous juxtaposi-tions of scheduling render aesthetic judgement based on a discrete individual work completely inappropriate. The general-ized values of 'newness' or 'darkness' in the work, were in turn incommensurate with the imprecisely recognized standing of 'the Bard'.

The shadow of Shakespeare ensured that the discussion would take the form of a cultural contest between television's role as a medium of entertainment and its responsibility as provider of education and induction into high culture. The assumed need to update the play was based on the populist construction of a mass audience, assumed to be ignorant of or impatient with ideas or styles of drama other than those of mass-market soap opera or police procedurals.

In these settings of mass education and high-volume cultural production, 'Shakespeare' becomes a sign of quality that is all the more effective because it has no precise referent. The work is stripped of the specificity of any language or history that might compromise the facility of its reproduction and becomes the flat field in which more or less inventive performances, providing more or less artistic pleasure, can be produced. The abstracted narrative of murderous conflict can be used to produce a historical allegory of our own violent times, setting the play in contemporary theatres of war.

Even more tellingly, the abstracted speeches that eloquently rehearse the horrors of tyranny, can be applied to the modern world. Antony Sher, who had presented a particularly powerful Macbeth in 1999, ended a TV documentary[22] about the pandemic of murder in post-apartheid South Africa with these lines:

> Alas poor country,
> Almost afraid to know itself. It cannot
> Be called our mother, but our grave,...
> Where sighs, and groans, and shrieks that rend the air
> Are made, not marked; where violent sorrow seems
> A modern ecstacy.

(4.3.166–72)

In Shakespeare's work, the lines are part of the scene at the English court that creates the turning point of the play. The murder of Macduff's family that Ross reports in this scene is turned into the occasion for the war that will topple Macbeth. In Sher's documentary, too, a particular incident, the murder of a young actor, is used as the entry point into a moving account of the terrible chaos that has overwhelmed the hopes for a free society after the injustices of racial division. Shakespeare could not have conceived of the particular mix of racial conflict, urban deprivation and a drug-fuelled gun culture described in Sher's documentary and Macbeth's feudal world of witch-belief and dynastic struggle offer only the broadest analogy for the terrors of life in the Southern Cape. Sher's ability to link the two, however, demonstrates the power of imaginative empathy that allows a King's Men play from the early seventeenth century to be transformed into a despairing image of hopelessness. It both honours and carries forward the seemingly timeless authority of the writer and his work.

Notes

INTRODUCTION: THE WRITER AND HIS WORK

1. See Samuel Schoenbaum, *Shakespeare's Lives* (Oxford: Clarendon Press, 1970) and Alan Nelson's regularly updated webpage http://socrates.berkeley.edu/~ahnelson/authorsh.html.
2. 'Out damned spot' was quoted most recently in an episode of the TV soap opera 'Hollyoaks' to characterize an affected would-be actress who brings pretentiously inappropriate material into pub entertainment.
3. Discussed in C.H. Herford and Percy and Evelyn Simpson, *Ben Jonson*, volume IX (Oxford: Clarendon Press, 1950), 13.
4. Ben Jonson, 'To the memory of my beloved The AUTHOR', in Stanley Wells and Gary Taylor, eds., *William Shakespeare The Complete Works* (Oxford: Clarendon Press, 1988), xlv.
5. This summary radically simplifies the extensive discussion of the text as well as three centuries of editorial practice. For a fuller account of the text of the play, see Stanley Wells and Gary Taylor, *William Shakespeare: a textual companion* (New York: W.W. Norton, 199). A careful reading of the textual notes and lists of emendations in modern editions will help the interested reader to be aware of the relationship between the text they are reading and the folio text.
6. See Richard Savage, 'Shakespearean Extracts from "Edward Pudsey's Booke"', Stratford upon Avon Note Books, no 1 (Stratford-on-Avon and London 1888). Lukas Erne, *Shakespeare as Literary Dramatist* (Cambridge: Cambridge University Press, 2003) discusses the evidence for Shakespeare's role in putting his plays into print.
7. See, for example, the uneducated heroine's reaction to *Macbeth* in Willy Russell's play *Educating Rita*, quoted in Alan Sinfield, 'Introduction', *New Casebooks Macbeth* (Basingstoke: Macmillan, 1992), 1.

CHAPTER 1   THE WORK AND THE STORY

1. The Folio text makes Banquo one of the kings with this direction: '*A shew of eight Kings, and Banquo last, with a glasse in his hand*'.

CHAPTER 2   THE WRITER'S TOOLS: ACTION AND LANGUAGE

1. Macbeth's lady is never referred to as 'Lady Macbeth' in the Folio text. She is variously 'Lady' and 'Queen'.
2. The banter is not included in all the early texts of *Romeo and Juliet*. The textual and theatrical implications are discussed in Jill Levenson (ed.) *Romeo and Juliet*, The Oxford Shakespeare (Oxford: Oxford University Press, 2000), 189.
3. D.P. Walker, *Spiritual and Demonic Magic from Ficino to Campanella* (London: The Warburg Institute, 1958), 113.
4. Ibid. 4.
5. There is a weather vane presenting an angel with a trumpet on the roof of Wilton house in Wiltshire. The house was owned by the Pembroke family, dedicatees of the First Folio. They entertained the King of Denmark at Wilton house in 1604 with the help of the King's Men, Shakespeare's company.
6. See Sinead Cusack's discussion of playing this scene in 'Lady Macbeth's Barren Sceptre' in Carol Rutter, *Clamourous Voices: Shakespeare's Women Today*, Faith Evans (ed.) (London: The Women's Press, 1989), 53–73.
7. Discussed in Wendy Wall, *Staging Domesticity: Household Work and English Identity in Early Modern Drama* (Cambridge: Cambridge University Press, 2002), 150.

CHAPTER 3   WORKING WITH IDEAS

1. See below 106–9; 124–6 for a discussion of the historical process by which these abstractions came to stand in for the play.
2. Though it is echoed with disastrous results in Cordelia's response to King Lear's request for assurance of her love. See *King Lear* 1.1. 95–105.
3. James I was the son of Mary Queen of Scots, executed by his predecessor, Queen Elizabeth.
4. See Brian P. Levack, *The Formation of the British State: England, Scotland and the Union 1603–1707* (Oxford: Oxford University Press, 1987, 188).

5. The sense of resolution in the play's finale has often been challenged in twentieth century reproductions that presented politics as a process of inescapable conflict. The most famous was Polanski's 1971 film in which Donalbain goes in search of the witches after Malcolm's victory, suggesting that the resolution was merely a temporary lull in a cycle of contested power.

6. See below 102 for a discussion of Shakespeare's relationship to the strand of political theatre being developed by the boy players in the hall theatres at the turn of the century.

CHAPTER 4   THE WORK IN HISTORY

1. The classic presentation of this critical practice was Cleanth Brooks's collection of essays, *The Well Wrought Urn* (New York: Reynal & Hitchcock, 1947), one of which, 'The Naked Babe and the Cloak of Manliness' provided a dense and complex appreciation of Macbeth's conscience soliloquy in 1.7.

2. For an account of Forman's writings, see Barbara Traister, *The Notorious Astrological Physician of London. Works and Days of Simon Forman* (Chicago: University of Chicago Press, 2001).

3. The text of Forman's notes is quoted from the transcription in A. R. Braunmuller (ed.) *Macbeth* (Cambridge: Cambridge University Press, 1997), 57–8.

4. See Lukas Erne, *Shakespeare as Literary Dramatist* (Cambridge: Cambridge University Press, 2003).

5. *The plays of William Shakespeare*: in eight volumes / with the corrections and illustrations of various commentators; to which are added notes by Sam. Johnson (London: R Tonson, 1765) stage direction 1.1.0.

6. The nearest analogy in Shakespeare is Lucio's speech in 1.2. of *Measure for Measure*. Scholars have speculated about the provenance of this episode and have used it both to date the play and to suggest that it was a later interpolation by Middleton. See John Jowett and Gary Taylor, '"With New Additions" Theatrical Interpolation in *Measure for Measure*' in Taylor and Jowett *Shakespeare Reshaped 1606–1623* (Oxford: Oxford University Press, 1993), 106–236.

7. J. Leeds Barroll, 'Shakespeare without King James' in *Politics, Plague and Shakespeare's Theatre* (Ithaca: Cornell University Press, 1991).

8. Ibid. 149.

9. Ibid. 150.

10. See William St Clair, *The Reading Nation in the Romantic Period* (Cambridge: Cambridge University Press, 2004), 696.
11. Ibid. 39–42.
12. See Roslyn Knutson, *The Repertory of Shakespeare's Company 1564–1613* (Fayetville: University of Arkansas Press, 1991), 111.
13. See Alison Shell, *Catholicism, Controversy and the English Literary Imagination* (Cambridge: Cambridge University Press, 1999), 142ff.
14. Jenny Wormald, 'Gunpower, Treason and Scots', *Journal of British Studies*, 24 (1985), 154.
15. Shell, *Catholicism*, 111.
16. Stuart Clark, 'Sights: King Saul and King Macbeth', in *Vanities of the Eye Vision in Early Modern European Culture* (Oxford: Oxford University Press, 2007), 236–65.
17. Michael Hawkins, 'History, Politics and Macbeth' in John Russell Brown (ed.), *Focus on Macbeth* (London: Macmillan, 1982), 161.
18. R. Doleman (Robert Parsons) 'A Conference about the Next Succession', in William C. Carroll, *Macbeth Texts and Contexts* (Bedford Books: Boston and New York, 1999), 196.
19. Quoted in Carroll, *Macbeth*, 204.
20. Levack, *Formation of the British State*, chapter 1.
21. Wormald, 'Gunpowder, Treason and Scots', *Journal of British Studies*, 24 (1985), 158.
22. Quoted in Carroll, *Macbeth*, 120. See also Levack, *Formation of the British State*, 195.
23. Nick Aitchison, *Macbeth, Man and Myth* (Stroud: Sutton Publishing, 1999), 107.
24. Holinshed, *The Chronicles of England, Scotlande, and Ireland* in Geoffrey Bullough, *Narrative and Dramatic Sources of Shakespeare*, Volume VII (London: Routledge and Kegan Paul, 1973), 495.
25. Ibid. 496.
26. Ibid. 496.
27. Ibid. 497.
28. Annabel Patterson, *Reading Holinshed's Chronicles* (London: University of Chicago Press, 1994) emphasizes the way that Holinshed's history is written to foreground ideas about constitutional kingship.
29. Holinshed, *Chronicles*, 498.
30. Christina Larner, 'James VI and I and Witchcraft', in Alan G. R. Smith (ed.), *The Reign of James VI and I* (Macmillan: London, 1973), 76.
31. There is a current critical consensus that additions to the play were made by Thomas Middleton. See the discussion below 98–101.
32. See below 128–31 for a discussion of the modern critical procedure that makes just those links.

33. C. Holmes, 'Women: witnesses and witches', *Past and Present* 140 (1993), 63.
34. Stuart Clark, *Thinking with Demons: the idea of witchcraft in early modern Europe* (Oxford: Oxford University Press, 1997).
35. See Kirby Farrell, *Play, Death and Heroism in Shakespeare* (University of North Carolina Press, 1989), 158.
36. See Bullough, *Narrative and Dramatic Sources,* 470–2.

CHAPTER 5 THE WRITER AT WORK

1. Details of these transactions are to be found in the numerous biographies of Shakespeare. The clearest detail is in Samuel Schoenbaum, *William Shakespeare: a Documentary Life* (Oxford: Clarendon Press, 1975).
2. See Katherine Duncan-Jones, *Ungentle Shakespeare: Scenes from his Life* (London: Arden Shakespeare, 2001).
3. Quoted everywhere but here from Samuel Schoenbaum, *A Compact Documentary Life* (Oxford: Oxford University Press, 1977), 151.
4. See Samuel Schoenbaum, *Shakespeare's Lives* (Oxford: Clarendon Press, 1970), 53–9.
5. Quoted and discussed in Schoenbaum, *Shakespeare's Lives,* 239.
6. See David Cook (ed.) *Dramatic records in the Declared accounts of Treasurer of the Chamber, 1558–1642* (Oxford: Malone Society Collections VI, 1962), 90–124 for a list of such routine payments.
7. Scott's imaginative representation of Elizabethan society in *Kenilworth* draws on *Macbeth* in a number of the chapter epigraphs and in its idea of a world in which there are 'intelligencers everywhere'. See Diana Henderson, *Collaborations with the Past* (Ithaca and London: Cornell University Press, 2006), 50.
8. 'To the Great Variety of Readers' in Wells et al., *The Complete Works,* xlv.
9. Michael Wood, *In Search of Shakespeare* (London: BBC Worldwide Limited, 2003), 175.
10. Michael Wood, *In Search of Shakespeare* (London: BBC Worldwide Limited, 2003), 164.
11. London: Jonathan Cape, 2004.
12. Bullough, *Narrative and Dramatic Sources,* 471.
13. Greenblatt, *Will in the World,* 332, (italics added).
14. Greenblatt, *Will in the World,* 334.
15. Ibid. 335.
16. See above, 56–7.
17. Stephen Greenblatt, Walter Cohen, Jean E. Howard, Katherine Eisman Maus (eds.) *The Norton Shakespeare* (London: W.W. Norton, 1997).

18. See Francis Barker, *The Tremulous Private* Body (London: Methuen, 1984); Gail Kern Pasteur, *The Body Embarrassed* (Ithaca: Cornell University Press, 1993); Jonathan Sawday, *The Body Emblazoned* (London: Routledge, 1995).
19. In Braunmuller, *Macbeth*, 58.
20. This mapping is, of course, neither comprehensive nor complete. The history plays include figures such as Joan of Arc, in *1 Henry VI*, whose successful pursuit of masculine, military roles, has her condemned as a witch. See Jean Howard and Phyllis Rackin, *Engendering a Nation: a Feminist Account of Shakespeare's English Histories* (London: Routledge, 1997).
21. See Aitchison, *Man and Myth*, 84–6.
22. Bullough, *Narrative and Dramatic Sources*, 506–7.
23. Discussed in Muriel Bradbrook, 'The Origins of Macbeth', in John Wain (ed.), *Shakespeare: Macbeth* (Basingstoke: Macmillan, 1968), 236–58, 244.

CHAPTER 6   THE WORK REWORKED

1. Asserted, for example, by the Archbishop of Canterbury, Rowan Williams in a public discussion that opened the Royal Shakespeare Company's Complete Works Festival on Shakespeare's birthday in 2006.
2. See Susan Brock and E.A.J. Honigman, *Playhouse Wills 1558–1642* (Manchester and New York: Manchester University Press, 1993).
3. Leonard Digges in the prefatory matter to Shakespeare's *Poems* (1640) in Stanley Wells and Gary Taylor, *William Shakespeare The Complete Works* (Oxford: Oxford University Press, 1988), xlviii.
4. Roslyn Knutson, *The Repertory of Shakespeare's Company* (Fayetteville: University of Arkansas Press, 1991), 169–70; 166.
5. *Macbeth* has been included in the Oxford *Collected Works of Middleton* (Oxford: Clarendon Press, 2007) with a full account of the textual evidence for his hand in the play.
6. Stanley Wells, Gary Taylor, John Jowett and William Montgomery, *William Shakespeare: A Textual Companion* (Oxford: Clarendon Press, 1987), 15.
7. For a contrary view see Lukas Erne, *Shakespeare as Literary Dramatist* (Cambridge: Cambridge University Press, 2003), 189–91.
8. The options are fully discussed in A. R. Braunmuller, (ed.) *Macbeth* (Cambridge: Cambridge University Press).
9. William St Clair, *The Reading Nation in the Romantic Period* (Cambridge: Cambridge University Press, 2004), 151.

10. Seen, for example, in the presentation of the witches in the anti-masque of Ben Jonson's *Masque of Queens* performed at court in 1608.

11. The Oxford *Middleton* gives this speech to Hecate, an editorial intervention with no justification in the Folio text of *Macbeth*.

12. See Knutson, *Repertory*, 12; 90.

13. Ibid. 90.

14. Thomas Middleton, *The Witch*, Elizabeth Schafer (ed.) (London: A&C Black, 1994), 1.2.18. For the source in Scot, see the note in Ibid. 13.

15. See 1.2.94–5.

16. Barnaby Rich, *The Honesie of this Age*, (1614) B3v-4r. Quoted in Braunmuller, *Macbeth*, 239.

17. Thomas Heywood, *The Late Lancashire Witches*, Laird H. Barber (ed.) (New York and London: Garland Publishing 1979). In the final witch sequence, a witch in the form of a cat appears, possibly reusing the cat costume from *The Witch*.

18. See, Mary Edmond, *Rare Sir William Davenant* (Manchester: Manchester University Press, 1987), 13–19.

19. Sir William D'Avenant, *Macbeth, A Tragedy*: With all the Alterations, Amendments, Additions, And New Songs. As it is now Acted at the Dukes Theatre London (Printed for A. Clark [etc.] *1674*).

20. Rebecca Rogers, Ph.D thesis, University of Southampton, 1998.

21. Richard Kroll, 'Emblem and Empiricism in Davenant's Macbeth' *ELH*, 57. 4 (1990), 835–64.

CHAPTER 7   A LASTING WORK

1. *The Diary of Samuel Pepys*, Robert Latham and William Matthews (eds.), (London: G. Bell and Sons Ltd, 1974), volume VIII, 7, 171.

2. John Downes, *Roscius Anglicanus* (1708), Judith Milhous and Robert D. Hume (eds.) (London: The Society for Theatre Research, 1987), 33. Downes first worked for Davenant shortly after *The Siege of Rhodes* (1657). Upon his retirement in October 1706, he began to write *Roscius Anglicanus: Or an Historical Review of the Stage*.

3. Thomas Duffett, *The Empress of Morocco. A Farce*. Acted By His Majesties Servants (London: Printed for Simon Neal, 1674).

4. See William Carroll, 'Two Truths are Told': Afterlives and Histories of Macbeths', *Shakespeare Survey*, 57 (2004), 69–80.

5. See J.C. Trewin, 'Macbeth in the Nineteenth Century', *New Theatre Quarterly*, 1.3. (1971), 26–31.

6. A useful summary of these changes is provided by a series of essays collected as 'One Play in its Time, No 1: *Macbeth*', *New Theatre Quarterly*, 1.3. (1971), 12–58.

7. Colin Franklin, *Shakespeare Domesticated: The Eighteenth Century Editions*, (Aldershot: Scolar, 1991).
8. *The Tatler*, no. 252, Thurs 16 November 1710.
9. Compare the discussion above 29–30.
10. William Richardson, *A Philosophical Analysis and illustration of some of Shakespeare's Remarkable characters* (London: J. Murray 1774), 74–5.
11. Ibid. 77.
12. See Simon Williams, 'Taking Macbeth out of himself: Davenant, Garrick, Schiller and Verdi', *Shakespeare Survey*, 57, 2004, 54–69.
13. Arthur Murphy, *The Life of David Garrick* (New York and London: Benjamin Blom, 1969), 71.
14. See Bartholomeuz, *Macbeth and the Players* (Cambridge: Cambridge University Press, 1969), 59.
15. Murphy, *Life of Garrick*, 83.
16. The glosses on the line in the Variorum edition show how Murphy was able to make scholarly controversy out of Garrick's enunciation of the line. See Horace Howard Furness, *A New Variorum Edition of Shakespeare* Volume II, *Macbeth* (Philadelphia: J.P. Lipincott & Co. 1873), 107.
17. Furness, *Variorum*, 98.
18. Murphy, *Life of Garrick,* 81.
19. Ibid. 83.
20. Ibid. 337.
21. See William St Clair, *The Reading Nation in the Romantic Period* (Cambridge: Cambridge University Press, 2004).
22. Thomas Cooke, *A Prologue on SHAKESPEARE and his Writings, Spoke by Mr Garrick, at the Theatre-Royal in Drury Lane*; printed with *An Epistle to the Right Honourable the Countess of Shaftesbury* (London: T. Cooper, 1743).
23. Theophilus Cibber from *Two Dissertations on the Theatre* (London, 1753), 56.
24. Murphy, *Life of Garrick,* vol. II, 15.
25. Ibid. 183.
26. See Lucy Hartley, *Physiognomy and the Meaning of Expression in Nineteenth Century Culture* (Cambridge: Cambridge University Press 2001), for an account in the Introduction of the codification of facial expression as a route into the mind and character of individuals.
27. Quoted in Jonathan Bate, *Shakespearean Constitutions: Politics, Theatre, Criticism 1730–1830* (Oxford: Clarendon Press, 1986), 35.
28. A.C. Bradley, *Shakesperean Tragedy* (London: Macmillan, 1969).
29. Ibid. 418–9.
30. Ibid. 419.
31. Furness, *Variorum* 162.
32. Sigmund Freud 'Some Character Types met with in Psychoanalytic work' in *The Pelican Freud Library*, volume 14 (Harmondsworth:

Pelican Books, 1985), 299–316.

33. Ibid. 301.
34. Ibid. 307.
35. Ibid. 308.
36. Ibid. 306.

CHAPTER 8   THE ABSTRACT WORK

1. William St Clair, *Reading Nation*, 347.
2. L.C. Knights, 'How Many Children had Lady Macbeth? An Essay on the Theory and Practice of Shakespeare Criticism' in *Explorations* (London: Chatto and Windus, 1946), 1–39.
3. Ibid. 3.
4. See Francis Mulhern, *The Moment of Scrutiny* (London: New Left Books, 1979); Richard Halperin, *Shakespeare Among the Moderns* (Ithaca and London: Cornell University Press, 1997), 38–41.
5. Janet Adelman, '"Born of woman": Fantasies of Maternal Power in Macbeth', in Alan Sinfield, *New Casebooks Macbeth* (Basingstoke: Macmillan, 1992), 53.
6. Ibid. 55.
7. Ibid. 57.
8. Adelman's text depends on Melanie Klein's adaptation of Freud's theories of the Oedipus complex to include relations with the mother as central to infant psychic development as well as Hélène Cixous's critique of Freud in 'The laugh of the Medusa' in trans. Keith Cohen and Paula Cohen, *Signs*, 1.4. (1976), 875–93.
9. Quoted in Paul Sheren, 'Gordon Craig and *Macbeth*', *Theatre Quarterly*, 1.3. (1971), 44–7.
10. See Geraldine Cousin, 'Footsbarn: From a Tribal Macbeth to an Intercultural Dream' *New Theatre Quarterly*, 9 (1993), 16–36 and Kathleen McLuskie, 'Macbeth\Umabatha: Global Shakespeare in a Post-Colonial Market', *Shakespeare Survey*, 52, 1999, 154–65.
11. Robert Little, 'Everyone likes Chocolate', *Vogue* (November 1, 1936), quoted in Rena Frayden, *Blueprints for a Black Federal Theatre, 1935–39* (Cambridge: Cambridge University Press, 1994), 153.
12. See Charles Marowitz, 'The Marowitz Macbeth', *Theatre Quarterly*, 1.3. (1971), 49.
13. Ibid. 47.
14. There is no space in this book to discuss film as a medium for the play. See Graham Holderness, 'Radical Potential: *Macbeth* on Film', in Alan Sinfield, *New Casebooks Macbeth* (Basingstoke: Macmillan, 1992), 151–60; Antony Dawson, 'Cross Cultural Interpretation: Reading Kurosawa Reading Shakespeare', in Diana Henderson (ed.), *A Concise Companion*

to Shakespeare on Film (Oxford: Blackwell Publishing, 2006).

15. Hugh Grady, 'Modernity, modernism and postmodernism', in Michael Bristol and Kathleen McLuskie with Christopher Holmes, *Shakespeare and Modern Theatre* (London: Routledge, 2001), 20–35.

16. *Macbeth* was included in the therapeutic experiment that took Royal Shakespeare company actors to Broadmoor to work with psychotic prisoners and 'in July 1998 by actor-director Hulugappa Kattimani as the centre-piece of a rehabilitation programme for the inmates of Mysore prison, most of who were serving life-sentences for murder'. See Murray Cox, *Shakespeare comes to Broadmoor* (London: Jessica Kingsley, 1992); Poonam Trivedi, '*Macbeth* in India', in Sonia Massai (ed.), *World Wide Shakespeares* (London: Routledge, 2005), 48.

17. *The Sunday Times* 13.11.05, 64.

18. *Times* 14.11.05, 27.

19. *The Observer* 13.11.05, 4.

20. *The Observer* 13.11.05, 4.

21. *Times* 19.11.05, 70.

22. Screened in July 2007.

Select Bibliography

EDITIONS

Macbeth, A. R. Braunmuller ed. (Cambridge: Cambridge University Press, 1997).

The Tragedy of Macbeth, Nicholas Brooke ed. (Oxford: Clarendon Press, 1990).

Macbeth Texts and Contexts William. C. Carroll ed. (Boston: Bedford St Martin's, 1999).

Macbeth, Inga-Stina Ewbank ed. in Thomas Middleton, *Collected Works,* gen. ed. Gary Taylor and John Lavagnino, 2 vols. (Oxford: Oxford University Press, 2007).

Macbeth, A New Variorum Edition of Shakespeare, volume II, Horace Howard Furness (Philadelphia: J.P. Lipincott & Co., 1873).

Macbeth, Stephen Greenblatt ed. in Stephen Greenblatt, Walter Cohen, Jean E. Howard, Katherine Eisman Maus, eds. *The Norton Shakespeare Based on the Oxford Edition* (New York and London: W.W. Norton and Company, 1997).

Macbeth, Kenneth Muir ed. (London: Methuen, 1984).

ADAPTATIONS

D'Avenant, Sir William, *Macbeth, A Tragedy*: With all the Alterations, Amendments, Additions, And New Songs. As it is now Acted at the Dukes Theatre London (Printed for A. Clark etc., 1674).

Duffett, Thomas, *The Empress of Morocco. A Farce.* Acted By His Majesties Servants, (London: Printed for Simon Neal, 1674).

Spencer, Christopher (ed.), *Davenant's Macbeth from the Yale manuscript: an edition, with a discussion of the relation of Davenant's text to Shakespeare's* (New Haven: Yale University Press, 1961).

FILMS

Joe Macbeth, dir. Ken Hughes (Columbia Pictures, 1955).

Macbeth, in *Shakespeare Retold* (DVD, London: BBC, 2006).

Macbeth, dir. Philip Casson (1978, reissued Watford: Thames Video 1991).

Macbeth, adapted and dir. Orson Welles (1948, reissued London: Second Sight Films, 1996).

Macbeth, dir. Roman Polanski (Caliban Films, 1971).

Macbeth on the Estate, dir. Penny Woolcock (London: BBC 1997).

Men of Respect, dir. William Reilly (Columbia Pictures 1990, reissued London: VCI 1996).

Scotland, Pa., dir. Billy Morrissette (Abandon Pictures, 2001).

Throne of Blood, dir. Akira Kurosawa (Connoisseur Video, 1957).

CRITICISM AND HISTORY

Adelman, Janet, *Suffocating mothers: fantasies of maternal origin in Shakespeare's plays* (New York and London: Routledge, 1992). A feminist, psychoanalytic account of Shakespeare's plays, including *Macbeth*.

Aitchison, Nick, *Macbeth, Man and Myth* (Stroud: Sutton Publishing, 1999). A thorough and readable account of the archeological and literary evidence surrounding the historical Macbeth.

Barroll, J. Leeds in *Politics, Plague and Shakespeare's Theatre* (Ithaca: Cornell University Press, 1991). An important critique of the received view about the relationship between Shakespeare's playing company and the court of James VI and I.

Brooks, Cleanth, 'The Naked Babe and the Cloak of Manliness' in *The Well Wrought Urn* (New York: Reynal & Hitchcock, 1947). An influential example of a close reading of the poetry in *Macbeth*.

Hodgdon, Barbara and Worthen, William, *A Companion to Shakespeare and Performance* (Oxford: Blackwell Publishing, 2005). A collection of essays that includes up-to-date analyses of the relationship between performances and texts of Shakespeare, including *Macbeth*.

Kliman, Bernice. *Macbeth*, Shakespeare in Performance series (Manchester: Manchester University Press, 1992). A useful account of the mainstream performance history of *Macbeth*.

Knights, L.C., 'How Many Children had Lady Macbeth? An Essay on the Theory and Practice of Shakespeare Criticism' in *Explorations* (London: Chatto and Windus, 1946). An influential essay on the symbolic meaning of image patterns in *Macbeth*.

Larner, Christina, *Enemies of God: The Witch-hunt in Scotland* (London: Chatto and Windus, 1981). The story of witchcraft in Scotland in Shakespeare's time.

Schoenbaum, Samuel, *Shakespeare's Lives* (Oxford: Clarendon Press, 1970). A fascinating and readable account of the way that the documentary evidence about Shakespeare was turned into the writer's life.

—— *William Shakespeare: a documentary life* (Oxford: Clarendon Press, 1975). Reprints the documents from the period associated with Shakespeare.

Sinfield, Alan, *New Casebooks Macbeth,* (Basingstoke: Macmillan, 1992). Brings together the 1980s revisionist views of the play.

Wells, Stanley and Taylor, Gary, with John Jowett and William Montgomery, *William Shakespeare: a textual companion* (Oxford: Clarendon Press, 1987). A comprehensive authoritative account of the textual problems in Shakespeare's plays including *Macbeth.*

Wood, Michael, *In Search of Shakespeare* (London: BBC Worldwide Limited, 2003). A popular biography of Shakespeare that was the basis of a widely admired television series.

Index

Printed in the United Kingdom by
Lightning Source UK Ltd., Milton Keynes
141483UK00001B/28/P